Teacher Success & Survival Secrets

101 Success & Survival Secrets to Empower Educators

Nothing is as rewarding as putting smiles on faces throughout the globe as an educator and illuminating impressionable minds to impact, shape and transform a generation.

Paul F. Davis

Invite worldwide speaker, life-changing author, and educational consultant Paul F. Davis to speak in your city. Encouraging administrators, educators, and students is Paul's passion.

info@PaulFDavis.com

PaulFDavis.com

Published by Dream-Maker Inc.

Copyright 2010 Paul F. Davis & Dream-Maker Inc.

All rights reserved. No part of this book may be reproduced or transmitted in any form or by any means, electronic or mechanical, including photocopying, recording, or by any information storage and retrieval system without written permission by the publisher, except solely for the purpose of a promotional book review wherein is permitted only a brief quotation.

Printed in the United States of America.

Library of Congress Cataloging-in-Publication Data
Davis, Paul F.

Teacher Success & Survival Secrets

By Paul F. Davis

Library of Congress Control Number:
ISBN 978-0-9826458-0-2

Warning – Disclaimer

The purpose of this book is to educate and entertain. The author or publisher does not guarantee that anyone following the techniques, advice, suggestions, tips, ideas, or strategies will become successful. The author and the publisher shall have neither liability or responsibility to anyone with respect to any loss or damage caused, or alleged to be caused, directly or indirectly by the information contained in this book.

Introduction

New and old teachers alike across the country are becoming disillusioned with the educational structure, overwhelmed by administrative requirements, and disgusted with their inability to discipline students. These challenges combined with being underpaid, rarely recognized, and under appreciated are sufficient causes for educators to seek employment elsewhere.

After being a new teacher myself and watching bright eyed new educators get the smiles wiped right off of their faces and look like they had just gone twelve rounds with the heavyweight champ of the world, I immediately knew some resource needed to be created to adequately prepare and empower new teachers for success.

Beyond the blood and urinalysis tests, fingerprints, contracts to prevent school board liability, teacher introductions, orientation days at the school district headquarters, tour of the facility where you will be teaching, data days and continuing education: what exactly is being done to genuinely and adequately prepare teachers to transition into the educational profession and succeed as educators?

As an educator who experienced this process firsthand, I can honestly say too little and not enough is being done.

My assigned mentor at the school where I taught had little time for me from day one and treated me more like an annoyance than a fellow educator in need of assistance. Obtaining a masters degree was mentioned and seemed to be her top priority.

I certainly don't fault her for it. How else can one survive with a career in education without ongoing personal investment to facilitate professional advancement? If I were in her shoes, I would have probably done the same thing to ensure my financial wellbeing and improve my career prospects.

From my perspective however (and for the purpose of this book to empower new teachers for success) my assigned teacher mentor was not proactive enough to truly help me. Perhaps my strong personality somewhat intimidated her and made her feel I was unapproachable.

As for me I was struggling to survive, sometimes feeling like I was sinking in quicksand from day one – not because the rigors of teaching were so challenging. It was all of the other stuff administration piled on me.

Undoubtedly educational administrators these days (as school board budgets are being cut by the millions) are overwhelmingly being stretched thin by their principals and understandably have difficulty coping with the many demands put upon them.

Surely there is only so much one administrator can do. Once the many tasks and assignments are piled high on top of them, eventually something is going to fall to the waist side and suffer. As a new teacher and novice to the nuances of working within the public school system, I felt I was neglected as a new teacher and not properly trained for the job as a teacher.

Certainly goodhearted and well-intentioned principals with miniscule school budgets also have limitations with how much they can do any given day, which often forces them to assign a multiplicity of tasks to mentors such as mine.

Know therefore that I am not demonizing anybody, because I sympathize with and respect everyone serving in the educational profession. I certainly would not dare or think to be an administrator as I am not so gifted, neither inclined. I therefore wholeheartedly honor every principal, administrator, and teacher serving within the educational system.

My small contribution and passion is to help new teachers successfully transition, not be overwhelmed, chewed up, or spit out by the grueling process that can be personally demeaning to any human being.

So as to adequately prepare new and veteran teachers alike to survive this process and succeed as educators, I have written this book. Please know as I write, I have malice toward none and charity for all.

Nevertheless to help teachers succeed as educators I must be somewhat truthful and call things as I see them (or rather experienced them as an educator myself).

Educators tend to have a particular and peculiar DNA to them. They like to be right and take pleasure in letting you know they are right. Hence they often radiate a degree of arrogance when they assert that which they know.

I was shocked to be scolded by a second year teacher who upon observing my handwriting during an informal teachers' meeting, reprimanded me as if I were a 2nd grade student.

I suppose her fragile identity was consumed with her job as a teacher, which after she survived and completed the first year of she now felt superior to the incoming teachers. I guess nitpicking me made her feel special. Nevertheless I'm glad I could be of service to build her frail self-esteem.

Thus longtime educators and administrators air of superiority sometimes immediately alienates many new teachers. Often the result is new teachers resort to acting like turtles. Certainly I could have become one of those who rarely stuck out his neck and asked questions. Yet that is not my style. As Patrick Henry said, "Give me liberty or give me death."

To walk on eggshells at your workplace is to die inside daily, something many educators do as they try to be forever compliant and fulfill all that is asked of them. I myself at times felt like I was dying inside as an educator. Yet never was this because of my students or the teaching occurring in the classroom. For me the major irritants and agitations came from outside of the classroom.

Whenever a new teacher feels ostracized and is made to feel that he or she does not fit in, it is a common response to feel inhibited and be more introverted in your dealings with others.

This was how I proceeded to navigate through my first year of teaching. By no means am I recommending such, nor am I saying my approach is right, neither should you necessarily follow it. Yet I survived and kept my sanity through the potentially diminishing experience by doing so.

Every personality and temperament requires a different response and approach. For me I chose to recoil and isolate myself a bit rather then become overwhelmed with the process. Moreover to prevent further discouragement, the last thing I wanted to do was burden my mentor by seeking her help.

I figured if I truly needed her help and she was able to assist me, she would make herself available and proactively communicate such to me. Furthermore I was a new teacher and needed some time to adjust. Too much too soon might push me over the edge. So I tried to keep a low profile while I was becoming acquainted to everything at my new job.

The computer operating system and the many websites I had to learn how to use were a bit overwhelming at first. Besides preparing lessons for my classes and endeavoring to harness unruly students disrupting my academic instruction, the hundreds of emails I received on my school provided laptop was a bit over the top.

Since I was taking courses for my educator professional development at night and a reading endorsement class at school during my planning period by day (as required by the principal to help our D grade school), I tried with everything within me to avoid taking on any more as I knew my limits.

To further complicate my life and new job, I was battling my insurance company and visiting doctors regularly to deal with all of the many problems caused by a drunk driver who totaled our family's only car during the summer just before my teaching job began. This drama continued from July until nearly the end of November during my first year of teaching. It couldn't have happened at a worst time.

Therefore whenever people shunned or gave me the cold shoulder, I counted it a blessing, realizing I had little time to suck up to people at work anyhow. I therefore outwardly showed humility, while inwardly not allowing others to belittle me.

I was shocked when one relatively new teacher, a second year teacher, criticized my handwriting and thought to scold me. I was laughing on the inside considering the extent of her insecurity that she so desperately was trying to assert herself and establish her identity as an educator. I just smiled as she berated me in front of a few of my peers, realizing her fragile self-mage might need a bit of recognition.

What hurt the most was my supposed mentor and administrators who rolled their eyes and made remarks behind my back, rather than taking the time to listen to me and seek to genuinely help me. Again "being right" was the order of the day and the hierarchical system enthroned within the school (and perhaps some school boards across the country where such was learned and passed down) was not very approachable.

The irony was when I applied for the teaching position everybody was super sweet and welcoming. All of that immediately changed after I was hired and everyone went into work mode. I certainly can appreciate and understand the many demands at hand facing administrators, leaving them little time to socialize and stroke fragile souls.

Yet if schools want to retain new teachers, some level of nurturing and affirmation must occur throughout the scope of employment for teachers. My principal (God love her) was a bit more of a drill sergeant than an encourager. I salute her for promptly telling us when the county was making a move economically that would affect us in some way and generously seeing that we got fed periodically thanks to the generosity of some local sponsors. However my heart yearned for a bit more meaningful interaction, guidance, and direction as an educator.

My principal visited my classroom three times over the course of the year, but never gave me any secrets or keys to improve my instruction. On the bright side my principal approved of my teaching and performance in the classroom.

The first meeting I had with my principal after beginning teaching wherein she somewhat evaluated teachers and gave guidance was when she asked to review our lesson plans. The primary focus was on having a lesson plan that met county school board guidelines.

When my first performance review took place in the principal's office, my teaching was deemed satisfactory and a stern exhortation to more often read my emails was given.

Ah yes! The overwhelming amount of emails were both amusing and annoying. Never mind the fact when I received a laptop for work nobody bothered to really tell me how to use the operating system and which emails were most important to read daily.

Thankfully, my nearby fellow ESOL (English to Students of Other Languages) teacher who had five years experience was gracious enough to kindly and patiently show me how to use the many operating systems and websites associated with all of the administration's ongoing requirements (which I suppose came from the county level, but were often a bit much).

As a new teacher I felt like I was choking to death on the overwhelming amount of emails, data, new computer systems, websites, and continuing education I was being required to take. All of these however were secondary to teaching six classes a day, which was my top priority.

Thankfully, I never let the secondary administrative duties get to me. In fact I often never got to many of the emails. The best I recall was having around 168 unread emails in my inbox. Usually however my unread emails were around 300. Not bad considering my unread emails upon beginning my employment were over 300 because I started work several days late due to being temporarily thought to be a sex offender (as two sex offenders in Illinois and Nevada have my same name, but a different birth date and physical appearance).

While I appreciate the county school board personnel investigator's thoroughness when it comes to ensuring sex offenders are not hired to teach, I felt it a bit much to prolong the investigation after the local police in Illinois affirmed it was not me and provided the website whereon the offender's photo was clearly visible (and obviously not me).

Yet were my child attending school, I too would want the same level of diligence and precaution to be exercised. Thank God somebody actually cares enough to do a thorough investigation to ensure our children's safety is upheld and guarded.

Within the classroom my students loved me, but I always believed the administrators and a handful of teachers (within the inner circle, who probably gossiped about me with the administrative hierarchy) weren't thrilled to have a new and needy teacher onboard. Nevertheless I happily remained clueless, kept a smile on my face, and moved forward along my merry way.

Sometimes being dumb in regard to certain things is the best and smartest thing you can do for yourself. New teachers need to know they will never please everybody. It is far better to attend to that which is important, rather than that which is urgent.

I therefore learned who were the power players on campus and swiftly read their emails daily. The assistant principal proved to be a good guy and consistently provided simple and clear instructions in his emails and directives. Many of the others thought they were clear, but weren't as articulate and skillful in providing concise instructions.

I royally screwed up when asked to proctor the FCAT during my first attempt, which quickly made me infamous on campus I'm sure. Yet the written instructions for ESOL students weren't as clear as they were for everybody else.

When I followed the drill sergeant's written green printout to the tee, I apparently blundered and should NOT have stopped the students at 11:20am for testing. Yet that is what I was told to do, follow the green script, which said stop.

I soon learned (much to the displeasure of my principal) ESOL students' FCAT exams are not to be timed. Perhaps had I shadowed a more seasoned educator through the process once, I could have more easily processed what I was to do. Nevertheless I was in over my head and getting a good taste of what it was like being an educator.

My ESOL students often complained about the insufficiency of the bilingual dictionaries they were given as a helpful "accommodation" to assist them in understanding vocabulary on the FCAT and tests. Apparently, many words on my ESOL students' tests were unable to be found within the dictionaries provided. I was surprised when I could not find the word "discrimination" within the Haitian Creole dictionaries.

Ironically, if not by reason of discrimination, Haitian Creole speaking students' dictionaries were nearly half the size of Latino Spanish speaking dictionaries. The Creole dictionaries were merely the "Concise" version, which the chair of our school's English department later agreed any parent upon first glance could recognize the blatant discrimination occurring. Certainly the Haitian students were getting the short end of the stick in this regard. I later would contact the NAACP about it.

Another expectation I quickly learned (understandably for a female dominated profession) was new teachers who are college educated should be able to read and understand what to do. It was remarkable what a mess the Florida Department of Education made of the FCAT instructions to begin with and how disheveled they were all strewn together, supposedly providing flexibility for each school to implement their own guidelines and criteria for testing.

Undeniably this visual learner found it a bit awkward and frustrating, but the hierarchy was not interested in any commentary so I kept my mouth shut and endeavored to conform to the best of my ability.

When my principal walked in at 11:20am and saw my ESOL students (predominately Haitian and Hispanic) talking incessantly and not testing, she was understandably livid. Yet I was diligently following the green instructional test handout told to be the proctor's guide to test giving, which said students were to be stopped at 11:20am. My principal however (which I later found out) wanted me to await her next instruction on the intercom (the voice of God as some called it) before stopping students from taking their tests.

So we had two testing scenarios going on (one for the "normal" kids and the other for the "ESOL students) and this new kid on the block was making a disaster of the FCAT for his students and his D grade school currently in discipline already with the county for poor academic performance.

Although I felt (and still feel bad for the principal and students who tested with me) a part of me has to laugh at the limited foresight given when I as a new teacher was assigned to proctor a test I had little knowledge of in the first place.

Nevertheless I achieved the distinguished recognition as being "the only teacher who couldn't follow instructions" on the FCAT (and I'm sure a bit more distinctions throughout my tenure of teaching). At least I took my bruises respectfully, nodded my head in agreement humbly, vowed to try to do better with sincerity, and marched onward into the battleground of academia.

Such are a few of my memorable experiences (and nightmares), which I have from my tenure teaching.

Nevertheless despite the old mindsets and decaying structures that seek to create educational conformists, a new breed of educators are arising to break the mold and pioneer a new frontier en route to revolutionary results.

For them I write these 101 (and then some) survival and success secrets. Any other extraordinary educator who is committed to be a lifelong learner may also come along and be hereby enriched with us.

Now let us begin and dive in to these gems to give you the winning edge as an educator.

Paul in India during a tour of schools in Chennai and Mumbai, where he encouraged youth to live their dreams, honor their parents and teachers, and purposefully pursue their passion.

Paul's inspirational talks to the youth made a tremendous impact and were a great source of strength to these youngsters, many who live in the poor nearby slums.

Paul actually lived in and traveled throughout India speaking across the vastly populated nation. Thus far Paul has visited India five times to fulfill speaking engagements.

1. Ask questions.

Asking questions will teach you many things, including help you quickly identify the perturbed and disinterested people in the school where you work. Let's face it, not everybody is overjoyed to be working as educators. Sometimes the frustrated fossils waiting for retirement are just serving their time, trying to get by and clock in their time until they meet their mark.

When you ask questions, note the reactions of people in the room and the administrators in power. Check out their facial expressions – rolling eyes, crinkled lips, frowns, lifting eyebrows, scratching heads, and the deadly evil eyes with the "How dare you for asking that!" look that tries to intimidate you.

The reactions of people are always revealing and telling. Asking questions also enables you to discover the managerial and educational philosophy of your principal and administrators. Many times the county has its own educational philosophy and mission statement, but this does not guaranty your principal and/or administrators willingly embrace and implement it.

You will learn over time to decipher the code with which your administrators speak. For example when I was hired, my principal often remarked how "enthusiastic" I was when she interviewed me. This was a signal to other administrators and athletic directors to actively recruit me for positions.

Truly there are no dumb questions, just dumb people who cowardly refuse to ask questions to which they don't know the answer. I would rather get answers to my questions than worry about what people think about me.

If people are condescending and look down upon you, they will do so with or without your leading. Therefore bypass such little hearts and big heads early on, by asking questions to gain information of use to you.

Paul at the Taj Mahal in India, home to a fifth of the world's populace and where the famous film "Slumdog Millionaire" was made. The food was quite spicy throughout India, but often very delicious. Nevertheless Paul had dysentery for the first two months of his nine-month journey, while living in curry land.

After much prayer and discretion with the fork, Paul managed to overcome the backlash from the spicy food (which often was enjoyable going down but fought back with a vengeance).

Like the humorous scene in the movie "Slumdog Millionaire", Paul often felt as if he was diving into dung as a teacher encircled by administrators who were bound and determined to make him a conformist. Nevertheless Paul somehow always managed to find his own way and escape.

For this reason Paul is able to write to you candidly today and hopefully put a smile on your face, while empowering you to survive and succeed as an educator.

2. Keep your mouth shut!

Keep your mouth shut, lest you prematurely and foolishly put your foot in it!

My first blunder in this regard came at a teachers' planning meeting, during which our school's reading chair and FCAT facilitator (and my mentor) was providing an example of an assignment we were required to complete. As I read her example on the overhead projector screen, I noticed at the bottom a book she mentioned she was currently reading by Bible teacher Joyce Meyer.

Having always heard about "separation of church and state" I got happily excited when I saw someone sharing their faith. Of course she was doing so in a more covert fashion via a book she was currently reading. Nevertheless my surprise got the best of me and sitting in my desk I suddenly said with a burst of energy, "Joyce Meyer!"

Unfortunately, I think my educational mentor took my response the wrong way and felt I may have been diminishing the author (and perhaps her). Actually it was quite the contrary as I respected the author and was happily surprised she was reading her material. Nevertheless, I had conveyed my surprise in such a way that much ambiguity and inaccurate perceptions were free to circulate. Incidentally, I don't know how comfortable my mentor felt around me after the incident.

I told my mentor after the incident that I liked Joyce Meyer and tried to make amends, but no relief of tension or mutual consideration every came. The damage had been done in a public setting and I possibly hindered her attempt to make a spiritual impact.

This made for a long first year teaching whenever I had to interact with my mentor, as she quietly seemed to go through the motions with me, but did never really connect and give of herself (I felt and perceived). Nevertheless I've been wrong before and misjudged people, but this was my perception.

I again tried to show my heart and support toward my mentor (through a reconciliation attempt) a week or so later by giving her a book I wrote titled *God vs. Religion*, but she never said anything whatsoever about the book thereafter. I speculated a bit about the sacred wall of separation between administrators and educators, which possibly she felt I breeched and perhaps therefore tried to keep me at arm's length.

Later in the winter when I heard through the grapevine my mentor was going through a divorce, I tried to be a blessing and discreetly give another book I had written titled *Breakthrough for a Broken Heart*, something I wrote after going through a painful divorce myself (although I did not mention the last part). The entire year I never received the slightest response from my mentor (who was also the Reading Coach at our school) about either book I gave to her.

That brings me to my third new teacher survival and success secret.

Paul speaking to youth about honoring their parents in East Malaysia across the island of Borneo.

3. Revere the Unspoken Wall of Separation.

If you get so fortunate and lucky to see an administrator smile and treat you like a human being, don't get too comfortable and friendly with them to falsely assume this will always be a reoccurring event. Familiarity can breed contempt. Therefore the astute administrator knows how to guard the professional relationship to sustain the level of respect to fulfill their role and the scope of their employment.

This delicate balancing act is one principals and administrators often fail miserably at navigating through, causing innumerable interpersonal problems (some even unbeknownst to them) and much friction at schools. Some will error on the side of being too friendly and have difficulty later enforcing policies and procedures. Others will be rigid, frigid, hard taskmasters that drive their staff away from them into corners to complain and gossip.

Neither scenario is advantageous to principals, administrators, and teachers. Despite all of these unspoken nuances and peculiarities, I tried to be a happy optimist. When at lunch I encountered a teacher and coach gossiping about the principal, I defended my principal and tried to give her the benefit of the doubt.

The teacher/coach doing the complaining had a horrible time adjusting (as he had moved to Florida from another state) and was suffering under a mountain of stress. He actually was later hospitalized because of migraines, something I never would have guessed for such a young and seemingly well-put-together man. I learned this because he himself told me.

I've always believed that if somebody will gossip to you, they will eventually gossip about you. That being said, I tried to keep a pure heart and carry on happily, realizing that I could never persuade anybody to like or forgive me if they chose to carry remorse.

As mentioned previously, several months after beginning teaching a fellow teacher told me my mentor was going through a painful separation. Upon learning of this news, instead of gossiping about it, I truly wanted to help encourage my mentor.

I therefore purposed to give her my book *Breakthrough for a Broken Heart* detailing how I overcame my personal pain during an unexpected divorce caused by my ex-wife's adulterous affair and unrepentant ways thereafter. After the following new teachers' meeting with my mentor, I politely passed the book to her privately when only the two of us were around and asked if maybe during spring break she could give me her literary opinion.

She never commented on the book and thereafter acted like the event never happened. By now, I determined not to ever approach any administrator for any reason, unless absolutely necessary. After my fumble with the FCAT in March a couple administrators at school, particularly the supplies coordinator (who was the most emotionless person I've ever met) and a few others, sometimes would not even return a greeting in the hallway when we passed each other. I later learned a few of the administrators were related to my mentor.

I received the cold shoulder and silent treatment by these special folks often when I greeted them. Thankfully, not every administrator was like this. As we got closer to the end of the school year, everybody started to get a bit more friendly and personable. I therefore reasoned any grumpy attitudes were not directed against me, but their life and job in general. That being said, thank God for "summer-cation" (as my baby brother used to call it when my mom was teaching).

To give you a geographical understanding as to the location of my classroom, I was located directly above the administrator's sacred quarters, upstairs in the media center. Sometimes this served me well with my students, because they were less unruly in the library than in other buildings. Although several would run through the media center when late to class, which angered the media specialist (a cool guy who rides a Harley Davidson and has a shaved head, not your typical librarian).

Sometimes the tension was profuse and acute in my building, almost like you could cut the atmosphere with a knife. I suppose the innumerable demands of the job were a bit burdensome at times for them. I therefore always tried to uphold my administrators in my heart. I'm certain I cannot fathom or imagine the extent of their many duties or sacrifice.

I recall hearing about all night affairs preparing for giving the FCAT and my teaching mentor arriving at school at 4:00am with an upset stomach to get the job done before the teachers and students arrived.

Despite the lack of joy I often encountered among coworkers, I nevertheless purposed to be polite, perky, and provide a smile to all passersby regardless of their response. I decided early on not to be depressed, nor dejected by the dead heads whose lack of response could have diminished me. Moreover I would remain respectful to my administrators, but never be fearful of or intimidated by them.

When the county school board deducted insurance payments from my check (which I did not authorize), I immediately politely protested (or so I thought) to my principal's secretary via email and asked for a prompt refund.

I had just been hit by a drunk driver in July and was desperately trying to pull together every last dollar to buy a new car, as my wife and I had been sharing rental cars after we lost our car. By the way, rental cars aren't always cheap in Central Florida, as pricing fluctuates based on how many conventions and tourists are in town. We spent over $800 in rentals one month (and that was at the cheapest place in town).

My principal's secretary could not have cared less about my dilemma. What she did care about however was my passionate requests (which she saw as demands), which she swiftly directed to the principal who promptly called me into her office for a "conversation" to tell me "that is not how things are done around here."

I bit the bullet and apologized, but explained my situation and desperate need of cash. A $386 monthly deduction for insurance (which I did not authorize) was not something I would easily tolerate and cowardly comply to given the miniscule salary of just over $2,600 net a month I was making after taxes for teaching. Not to mention I commuted a total of nearly 80 miles roundtrip to and from school, waking up at 4:45am to be there by 6:45am to begin work. By the end of the year I had put around 11,000 miles on my car.

Biting my lip and tongue became a normal practice rather quickly, as I soon learned any communication apart from "Yes, Ma'am!" wasn't kindly received. Hence I learned to revere the sacred wall of separation and all of those on the other side serving the hierarchy.

I felt like I was having a flashback and faintly hearing a Ukrainian taxi driver in my mind (who didn't manage to persuade me at the airport to take a ride with him in Kiev) walking away saying, "Fyak you Duke!" (my nickname, which he heard from my brother who was with me) all over again.

Don't let the uncertainty of whether or not "they" (the administrators) like you or not weary you. Giving into this form of manipulation and the silent treatment is exhausting. Guard your heart. Be good to yourself on the inside by staying positive and speaking well, while cultivating the winner within.

Never demean yourself based on uncertainties you know nothing about, which 90% of the time is worry paying interest in advance on something you most likely will never own. Believe the best about yourself and let the law of attraction work for you!

4. Don't bite off more than you can chew.

When I was first assigned to my room, I noticed I had two whiteboards, one of which I was told I could not write on because it was not erasable. The only problem was the main whiteboard located in the center of the class was the one I was told I couldn't write on, as it was a "smart board."

My first reaction understandably therefore was to ask, "How does this whiteboard (correction 'smart board') work?" I was told there was some special technology necessary to use it and I was instructed to contact the tech guy on campus who was in charge of all of that.

Upon contacting the "tech guy", the good fellow was up to his eyeballs in work dealing with the administrators and students computer network. I therefore didn't bother him and gave him some space. He told me he would get to it when he could and had the time.

Eventually when the tech guy (also a dean ...and there were so many deans I couldn't keep all of them straight as to their exact assignments) came to my room to finally assess the situation, he informed me that there were some missing components and parts needing to be acquired before I could begin to use the smart board. I certainly understood these things weren't cheap and therefore let it go, hoping and trusting one day I would be able to use my smart board.

Two months prior to the end of my first year teaching (at the writing of this book), I have never been contacted further about the acquisition about these necessary components to make my classroom's smart board operational.

When a doctorate professorial type made her rounds at our campus to "help" and asked me what she could do to improve my classroom experience, I replied: "You can give me a white board that works and ask the powers that be to do whatever is necessary to fix it."

My beloved mentor by the side of the "doctor" visiting my classroom obviously didn't like my response and mentioned I had "dropped the gauntlet". My remark, which was nothing more than a plea for help, was interpreted as a challenge for combat (not my intention).

So my time with administrators seemingly has been a battle every step of the way. As for the necessary components to improve my classroom and provide equal access to my English language learners, they never came.

I guess administrators and senior educators' egos are more important than the instruction of my students. Nevertheless I happily made do with the one white board I had in the room and pressed on with a positive attitude.

Had I continued to press on and persevere for the smart board, I might have got the ax and been fired. When I sent a couple emails weeks later in the fall (as a reminder) about a "dumb teacher with a smart board", hoping to amuse and prompt someone to attend to the needs of my classroom, nobody took action to improve the situation.

Hence I gladly made the most of it and attended to more important matters, not wanting to irritate my administrators. Besides my printer in the room didn't work either (nor did it the nearly the entire year until the last two weeks) and I was beginning to get used to this modus operandi at the beloved school where I taught English language learners (ELLs) from afar. I suppose ELLs weren't their top priority and could wait.

Ironically, upon doing some research online I discovered rule 6A-6.0904 within the administrative legal code in Florida providing *Equal Access to Appropriate Instruction for English Language Learners*, legislation passed in May, 2009, near the completion of my first year teaching. After receiving my final paycheck from my county school board (and former employer), I filed some of these matters with the Florida Department of Education to protect ELLs across the state and ensure they (and their teachers) are provided equal access.

Paul at Borobudur temple in Java, Indonesia preparing to get nasty & show his martial arts ability on any possible intruders who might dare to "drop the gauntlet" in his powerful presence within the citadel. An impenetrable stronghold and fortress sometimes needs some humor to transcend and help us. Invite Paul to your campus to disarm and diffuse the tension.

Remember your success as a new teacher will be determined not as much as what you say yes to, but more what you say no to.

It is far better to be faithful in a little and do it well than undertake and commit to do much but do it poorly. Sometimes the more you commit to, the more you befuddle the other more important things you were hired to do.

Schools have unlimited and countless queries and requests for help. Most of them are good and genuine requests that truly could benefit from a helping hand wherever they can get it. Yet it is important to remember that "good" is often the enemy of that which is "best" and most important.

Beware of saying yes prematurely to urgent pleas for help, before you assess what you are already doing and committed to. Your personal wellbeing, family, and health should always come before all of the volunteer tasks the school solicits help for.

Endeavor to maintain a balanced life lest you over do it and burnout before you begin. New teachers often have innumerable educational requirements and classes at night (or during the weekends) to take. Attend to your educational professional development first, before being the eager beaver who overextends himself.

Opportunities to serve will always be available. Relax. Take a deep breath. Attend to that which is paramount and most important before allowing yourself to be emotionally pulled upon and yielding to that which will thwart your professional progress.

Master what is in front of you and what you are contracted to do – teach. Thereafter once you feel like you are on top of your game, proceed to look for additional responsibilities (if that is your thing) and ways to serve.

5. Say No, or Nothing Often

One way to keep your sanity, avoid unwanted conflict, misunderstandings, and prematurely committing to something you are unfamiliar with; is to kindly say no, or simply say nothing at all.

The quickest way to reach exhaustion, burnout, and have a mental breakdown is to allow others with good intentions to persuade you to do more than you are capable of. You will get many emails as a new teacher (more than I could ever respond to), but that doesn't mean you have to reply to each and every one of them.

Sometimes the best response is no response. Often when you reply saying no, you will get another reply back asking you why not? Then you open the door for ongoing discussion, solicited explanation, and possibly some mild interrogation into your personal life.

Guard your personal life and affairs. Beyond your teaching contract hours, you have no obligation to disclose or do away with your personal time. As a human being you too are allowed to have a bit of a life and keep some time for yourself.

If you don't, you are likely to grind down your every last nerve and become bitter toward teaching altogether. Fundraisers and athletic events don't have to have you to succeed. If you don't feel inclined to help, kindly decline the offer or ignore the query lest you open up an emotional exchange whereby you might begin to feel guilty for saying no.

Don't get me wrong educators and administrators who work six and seven days a week (along with 12 hour days) are awesome people. I just want you to know, that lifestyle doesn't have to be you unless you willingly embrace and welcome it.

If you are single and have no social life or hobbies, perhaps all of these opportunities to serve will be a wonderful experience for you. If it works for you, go for it!

Yet not everybody jumps for joy at the chance to give away their Saturday after teaching unruly and boisterous kids all week long.

If you are full of resurrection power, enjoy the school staff, and have the spirit to help; you will be a gem highly valued by administrators and educators. For job security, this certainly is one way to solidify your teaching career and make yourself an MVP at your school.

The one time I screwed up the most was during the FCAT (the worst time to mess up). I had a room full of students, but half of them were not typically in my daily classes. Hence I had to quickly establish authority, connect with the kids, and try to govern the classroom.

Undoubtedly this is far easier when you are with students whom you already have an established rapport with than trying to regulate students who are unfamiliar with you. Nevertheless I did well, until I followed the faulty written instructions for the FCAT, which required test taking to stop at 11:20am. I erred in not allowing the ESOL students to keep taking their exam, which was not to be timed.

Thankfully, I called for a dean in the hallway monitoring the building and bathroom breaks. She kindly got me back on track and eventually administration stepped in (thankfully for the students) to correct the error. Unfortunately the dean that helped me that dreadful day later had to resign when she was alleged to have gotten involved relationally with a student.

After my FCAT blunder, I became the black sheep on campus to a few administrators and select teachers in the inner circle. Nevertheless I continued to teach my classes and excel in motivating many new students who had just arrived from overseas (no easy task when parents uproot kids against their will and bring them to another country).

6. Develop Your Own Teaching Style

As a new first year teacher, I expected to shadow other established teachers and find my way as an educator by modeling the proven experts in the field.

However because I taught ESOL students learning English as a second language, implementing a particular teaching method per say of another proven educator would not necessarily work for me. As unfortunate as this may be, it was true for me.

I therefore had to quickly discover and implement a successful teaching strategy that worked for me. I quickly learned that more important than my teaching methodology was to know the students I was teaching.

I was assigned and given the 11th and 12th grade ESOL students. Since the State of Florida's Department of Education does not fail students because of language barriers and challenges, many students at a fourth or fifth grade English level were in my high-school class.

The fact that they were unable or unwilling to read in English was not to be a barrier for them learning. Imagine this scenario. I the white man (who immediately gets stereotyped by Haitian and Latino kids as being aloof and not understanding their plight) was supposed to teach these students, who the previous year had an ESOL teacher who spoke Spanish and let them watch movies everyday (according to the students).

I guess this is why my predecessor was fired and I was hired. When my principal told me I would be teaching the 11th and 12th grade English book and curriculum to ESOL students (as mandated by the county school board), I basically agreed and said, "Yes Mam" and went to it.

I had no previous experience or knowledge as to my inability, as I had always succeeded everywhere else in the world teaching ESOL kids. Not to mention I had experience with Latinos and Haitians because I had traveled to nearly all of their countries, which the exception of Guatemala.

My Haitian students were happily surprised to learn I had been to their country and new some French words. My Latino students were thrilled to know I could speak a fair bit of Spanish (having studied the language in high-school, college, and University).

Moreover they were a bit amazed to learn I had been from Mexico to Argentina and was intimately familiar with most of their countries, having traveled numerous times to several of the countries.

Thankfully my travels, language ability, and entertaining teaching style enabled me to quickly establish rapport with my students. Keeping a sense of humor throughout the year enabled me to keep my sanity, especially when a new student arrived from overseas who could hardly speak a word of English.

I was so happy to see one student named Jesus, begin to embrace the English language and lay down his inhibition to reading in class. When Jesus arrived to class in the beginning, he would never participate in reading exercises.

However as a result of our fun and lively class conversations, eventually Jesus jumped into the mix and began to read a sentence or two with my help. We all gave Jesus a round of applause after the first time he read. I was so proud of Jesus and nearly cried right there in class.

Juggling assignments, teaching methodologies, and grading assessments for students of widely varying English levels was certainly challenging. Nevertheless I somehow intuitively and instinctively discovered my own teaching style, which obviously worked, as I was able to motivate my students (who were extremely lazy and resistant in the beginning) to do their assignments.

Don't feel obligated to be like everybody else. A square peg will never fit in a round hole. Other teachers and faculty may judge you, but until they have had to walk a mile in your shoes, do not feel obligated to conform to their methodology.

Certainly listening and observing more seasoned teachers will give you ideas and strategies to incorporate into you own teaching style. Yet in my opinion, your teaching style will have to be somewhat modified to work with the students you are given within the classroom.

Considering my own scenario mentioned above, it is safe to say no rigid and frigid by the book teaching methodology would work. These Haitian and Latino students were chewing up and spitting out many of their teachers daily, which was evident by the haggard looks on so many of the educators faces around me.

Our school had 45% or more of Hispanic students and 40% African American (within which the Haitian students were classified). The racial mix made for a fun cross-cultural experience for this world traveler. Yet when I first took the job, which was in another county other than the one where I live, I really had no idea as to the racial demographics.

My classroom composition as an ESOL teacher consisted of about 85% Latinos and 15% Haitians. We had a lot of fun and we undeniably learned a lot together. My students taught me as much as I taught them.

Whenever I heard a word in Spanish that intrigued me, usually at least once a month, I would ask the student to tell me what that word meant in English. Than I, like my students struggling to learn English, would repeat the word a few times in Spanish (during which the students would laugh and work with me to correct my pronunciation). After I mastered the pronunciation to the approval of my students, I would say in Spanish to whichever student(s) helped me learn the word: "Gracias, maestro(s)!"

This simple role reversal showed my students that I am not too proud to learn their language. Moreover as we did it in playful fashion, the exercise exemplified truly how languages are best learned – in a playful and carefree manner.

My own childlike mannerisms and ability to laugh through the learning process put the students at ease, while endearing them to me.

Through deepening and establishing a strong bond with my students, it was easier to lead them as their teacher. I wasn't necessarily predetermining strategically to accomplish this. It just simply came to me naturally as I in a playful manner enjoyed the interaction with my students, treating them as equals and human beings.

I understand my students' language challenges, as I have been to many of their countries and struggled myself with their own respective languages. That being said, it is worth noting that Latinos all do not speak Spanish the same way.

The Colombians are quick to point out that Puerto Ricans butcher the language. I would not say or write this had not my Puerto Rican students agreed and told me they create words. Some Puerto Ricans even went so far as to say their version of Spanish is a bit ghetto at times.

It was interesting and fun to see the rivalries between nationalities among Latino students. The typical white American educator would never think or recognize such a rivalry, but assuredly it does indeed exist. I got to see it firsthand when teaching these different nationalities within my ESOL class.

Considering all of these cultural nuances and cross-cultural challenges, not to mention the wide variety of language levels within my classroom (depending on how long ago ESOL students arrived in the country, some just weeks ago); it made for a very unusual heterogeneous classroom to teach. Hence I suggest educators adapt and apply their own teaching style.

7. Connect Before You Communicate.

Sometimes before you endeavor to drive home a point or teach a concept, you first have to connect with your students. Accessing background knowledge, telling a relatable story, and asking probing questions to set the stage for the lesson are all wonderful ways to connect with your students.

By first connecting with your students, you build a bridge to cross over and elegantly transition into the learning material. Nobody likes to be force fed anything, educational material included.

Given the social element of Latin and Haitian culture, I learned over time I could accomplish more with my students if I would first connect before trying to communicate educational concepts.

The visual learners in the classroom often responded to lessons and assignments like I would to my administrators' emails. "What am I supposed to do?"

They didn't want to read it, or when they did read it they had a mental block. The assignment had not yet sunk in, that is just what exactly they were required to do.

When I watched a show on the human brain and how it works, I learned that there are grooves within our brains according to the extent of the stimuli we receive. The more of a specific and certain stimuli you receive, the deeper the groove becomes. Therefore when a new assignment and concept is brought before a student (or educator in response to administrators' requirements), it is quite natural to first have a bit of mental resistance and perplexity.

It is a bit like African children in some of the poor remote villages I visited when serving as a missionary and humanitarian aid worker. When given American candy for the first time, which is stronger than what they are used to, African children often taste it for a while and then spit it out of their mouths.

This response is indicative to their inability to take in the unusual and overbearing stimuli (in this case upon their tongues). It is no different academically when students deal with new concepts, truths, and mental challenges within a classroom assignment.

Some students by reason of use are more apt to quickly embrace and respond to the challenge. Others on the other hand are a bit more averse to learning new things and tackling assigned exercises beyond their comfort zone.

Certainly as we grow older in years it is a known fact that adults do not as easily learn new material. For this reason most skilled and wise educators encourage parents to teach their children foreign languages while they are still young.

As teachers we can overcome students' aversion to new material by being patient and repeating in different manners the same instruction until students "get it". The mental light bulb will turn on for students at different times.

In my classrooms, I had a few gregarious and social Haitian students that sometimes struggled grasping the assignment and what was required of them. I found over time they best "got it" when I broke it down and humorously illustrated the point (almost like an actor) in front of them.

We would all have a laugh, feel refreshed, and they would happily proceed to do the assignment with a new level of enlightenment. Truly humor is a wonderful way to connect with students, win their trust, get them to like you, and enthusiastically put their heart into whatever they do for you.

In conclusion, don't be afraid to take some time to connect whenever you communicate. You never lose time when you take time to connect. In fact you actually save time because you increase students' understanding and performance.

8. Access & Activate Background Knowledge.

Youth have a wonderful array of real life experiences from which to pull from to easily relate to whatever you are teaching, but you have to elicit and access that background knowledge.

Asking questions, telling stories, and asking some more questions gives students a chance to adequately relate instances from their own lives. This then enables them to make vital and key connections when endeavoring to learn new educational material.

Activating students' background knowledge does not need to be a top-heavy experience. I find it works far better if it is done in a playful and fun manner, where learning is exciting and enjoyable.

For example, if you are teaching geography you can ask students which countries they have traveled to. Then once some students begin to speak up, you can ask them to share an experience from their travels that relates to your topic of discussion.

This type of discussion and classroom interaction awakens students to the joy of learning. When learning becomes more experiential, it becomes more memorable.

The problem with modern education is from the school board to the administrators to the educators the mandate has become conformity to state standards and criteria. This rigidity tends to choke the lifeblood out of meaningful education altogether leaving us with merely a lifeless structure.

So educators become strict conformists, alienate their students, but fulfill their dutiful requirements to keep their jobs. It seems in such an educational system there are more losers than winners and innumerable casualties along the way.

Those who suffer most are the students because their teachers become walking dead people with little heart and life in them. When educators stop building students through meaningful interaction and start barking at them to stay on track with the mandated academic discipline of the day, the human component is lost and students become angry.

When students get frustrated and angry, eventually they pull back emotionally and begin to rebel. Kids can see through hypocrisy and beyond the belligerent bulldog educational system's inflexible philosophy.

Students eventually weary under such an educational approach and become irritated with the tendency of educators to try to stay on track at the expense of dehumanizing them as persons.

Life is not easy as it is for many of students who come from broken homes with divorced parents. Economic challenges often demand that students' parents work two jobs to pay the bills and survive financially.

Other times students nowadays live with aunts, uncles, and elder siblings, while their parents live and work elsewhere. The complexities at home (often untold by students or unaccounted for by teachers) can be a reason why many students struggle academically in the classroom.

It is not uncommon for students to be working a part-time job after school for eight hours to help their parents pay the bills. When students come home late at night after work and are exhausted, the last thing on their mind is doing homework.

The high school where I taught began at 7:00am, which meant students had to be up by 5:30am to catch the bus by 6:00am in some instances. Some cultures don't typically go to bed before midnight. Students' tendency to follow the pattern of their parents often had to be altered in order to get an adequate amount of sleep before school began. Yet what goes on at a child's home, educators will never fully know.

One of the ways teachers can bridge the gap and build rapport is to provide open-ended questions that provide for meaningful classroom discussion. I also employed essay writing on topics of interest for my students, which works better to encourage students to speak on more sensitive subjects – subjects they might not want their classmates to know.

The first essay I had my students write was about their lifelong dreams. I wanted each student to tell me his or her dreams for the future. This essay always seemed to evoke a wonderful response from students, who thoroughly enjoyed revealing their personal passions and lifelong pursuits.

I built great rapport with my students by just asking for such information and genuinely getting to know that which is important to them. I even gave my students some extra credit for taking a 3 x 5 card and writing their dream on it, along with a picture of what the fulfillment of their dream will look like.

Each student put their picture on the card, wrote their dream down, and placed an image of the profession they dream to do or person they desire to be.

Periodically throughout the year whenever students became weary in well doing, I reminded them of their dream and encouraged them to continue to be disciplined in route to its fulfillment.

I thereby accessed my prior knowledge about my students (pertaining to their lifelong dreams) to motivate and activate their learning skills when necessary. It worked wonderfully! I am happy to say, every one of my students (some of which failed other classes) passed my ESOL class and learned a great deal of the English language along the way.

Find your own way to access and activate students' background knowledge. Incorporate your students' hobbies and interests into your lectures and lessons. As you do students will more willingly buy into and embrace the educational process.

Precious school children in Mumbai and Chennai, India who intently listened to Paul's inspiring messages and responded enthusiastically inviting him back again!

Paul with Colonel Ammerman and military chaplain to whom he spoke in Dallas, Texas at a national conference for distinguished officers serving our nation throughout the world.

9. Breathe Life into the Curriculum.

Whatever subject you teach, passionately breathe life into the curriculum. Find ways to make the learning material and focus relevant for students. Build bridges students can cross and become meaningfully engaged in the subject material.

Schoolwork without oxygen and air is dead letters, boring assignments, and drudgery. Be the living soul center stage in the classroom that intercepts and intersects the curriculum and the need for a captivating presentation.

Happily, intelligently, and skillfully reconcile the two so students can feel you when you teach. Emit a fragrance and aura that embodies the spirit of the material versus being merely overcome by the assignment itself.

Simplify the text when necessary through paraphrasing and summarizing so your students grasp the main idea. Otherwise it will go right over their heads and be a dead lesson that transmits nothing to them.

Make education lively and a part of students' lives. Why is it that educators present education and school lessons as monotonous tasks and drudgery? Where did we as teachers go wrong? What brought about this paradigm shift?

The answer to these questions should cause us to probe deeper and further evaluate the entire educational system as a whole. Perhaps this is a discussion worthy of another book altogether. If you have some answers and ideas to those questions, please write me at RevivingNations@yahoo.com. I'd love to hear from you. Testimonials from this book are also welcome.

Always remember the purpose of education is to prepare students for life. Education may be an educator's life, but for students the lessons must be full of life to be memorable.

Paul at the Grand Floridian Hotel at Walt Disney World during the Christmas holidays enjoying the decorations and delightful spirit of the season.

Paul with police officers in Jakarta, Indonesia at the airport en route to the tsunami epicenter where 200,000 people died.

10. Discipline Disrespectful and Unruly Students.

One of the strengths of the high school where I taught was the disciplinary measures and procedures by which our staff effectively dealt with and restrained inappropriate student behavior. We implemented something called "choice", where if students misbehaved they were sent to the dean's office.

After a student took a trip to the dean's office, their parents were immediately contacted. Following a student's third trip to the dean's office, they were suspended for a day of school. Repeat infractions eventually were dealt with by completely expelling and removing a student from the privilege of attending school altogether.

I heard from some of my fellow teachers (during lunch) that other high schools in the county had less strict disciplinary procedures, which led to pandemonium in the schools and blatant disrespect of teachers. Thankfully, discipline was one area in which our principal excelled. Despite our school being under discipline for poor performance academically (for the preceding year before I arrived), we excelled athletically and interacted on campus respectfully (although not perfectly). This was a huge accomplishment, because social skills are vital to students' success in life following graduation.

Maintaining a proper level of self-respect for yourself and others is paramount to getting along and getting ahead in life. As a teacher some of the disciplinary tactics I employed to harness my students and get them to cooperatively stay on task were the following.

First, I would try to call the students out by name and acknowledge their misbehavior and disruption of classroom progress, asking them politely to restrain themselves.

Secondly, I would relocate the student to sit elsewhere in the classroom (usually away from their friend, who was disrupting them or being disrupted by them). Thirdly, I would take the student outside and speak to them privately. Fourthly, if all else failed, I would call for a dean to have one of the administrator's come get the student and take them to the dean's office for discipline.

The deans at my high school were all awesome and very helpful. Without the disciplinary structure set in place, I'm sure it would have been a nightmare trying to teach my students. Thankfully, our principal from day one encouraged all teachers to call for a dean whenever they needed one.

Unlike some principals and administrators who don't want to be bothered, our disciplinary procedures were set in place to remove the bad apples and facilitate ongoing rigorous learning for the other students present in the classroom.

One of my fellow teachers with whom I often ate lunch recognized the usefulness of being able to call for a dean as needed to remove an unruly student. He was a mathematics teacher (algebra I believe) and needed the utmost concentration free from disruptions to adequately be able to teach students how to derive proper calculations, utilize formulas, and arrive at solutions to problems.

Understandably so, given the tedious nature of the subject, this teacher swiftly dealt with and disciplined bad attitudes as much as he did poor behavior. The result was his students were well mannered and cooperative in class for the majority of the time. On the rare occasion when a student would speak disrespectfully or make obscene gestures at the teacher, he without hesitation would call for a dean to remove the student.

I myself did not use as stringent a disciplinary policy (being a bit more easy-going myself), but when I discerned students were getting out of hand I did not hesitate to call for a dean to remove the unruly student(s).

Because of the nature of my subject, I welcome students to get a bit more gregarious and use the language. Therefore it is advantageous to align your disciplinary policies and implementation style according to the rigors of the subject that you are teaching.

Know however that whenever a student is getting on your nerves and thwarting your academic progress as a teacher, he or she has to be swiftly confronted and dealt with lest the whole class lose their focus.

Trust me I understand what it is like being the class clown and the motivations for pursuing such a status among students. I myself was voted "the funniest" in my high school class, much to the dismay of some of my former high school teachers who I no doubt disrespected and annoyed at times.

Sometimes by just sharing a brief laugh with your students you remind them that you are human, enabling you to again reconnect with them, before you proceed to communicate the daily learning task to focus upon.

Fifthly, another wonderful means by which to discipline your students is to involve their parents. Make a phone call to your student's parents and speak to them about the problem.

Complement their child for his or her positive qualities, but simultaneously express your concern for their poor behavior and how it is negatively affecting the entire class.

I don't recommend this, but once I even picked up my cell phone during class and phoned a student's parent. The student rarely gave me any problems after that. I suppose the embarrassment was sufficient to persuade the student to behave himself. Immediately his rude behavior stopped.

My mother (a retired veteran teacher of thirty years) learned from my dad how to embarrass an unruly student seeking attention in class. This method quickly diffuses the attention seeker when they feel the pain of becoming a laughingstock, rather than being praised for their bad behavior.

Basically, by being alert to each student's "hot buttons" and motivators you can employ innumerable tactics to get students to cooperate.

One of my quiet underperforming students suddenly took a shine to doing well in class when I relocated him to sit next to an attractive young lady who earned As in my class. I also gave the young lady a bit of extra credit for peer teaching. This was a wonderful win-win situation for all involved.

These are the type of creative problem solving methods that cannot be taught, but must be intuitively caught in the midst of the moment as you discern that which motivates and moves your students.

On the other hand, when a male student began to make sexual and crude comments to one of my female students, I immediately sent him to the dean to be disciplined for such behavior. Sexual aggression, be it verbal or physical, should not be tolerated in the classroom or anywhere on campus.

In another incident, two students began to speak filthy toward another young lady, while she was bending over to pick up her pencil. One of the young men tried to poke his pencil between her legs as somewhat of a joke. The young lady did not receive it well and I consequently called the office for a dean to remove the young men. When the principal arrived and heard the chain of events, she was not impressed to say the least.

Discipline is vital because as a teacher gaining your students' respect is far more important than trying to be liked. What good is it to be "liked" if students disrespect and walk all over you? Therefore the first couple of months in the classroom, a teacher needs to be a bit of a drill sergeant and sometimes a bulldozer when it comes to driving home class rules and punishment for infractions.

Our school had police officers on campus, which we could promptly call to assist in dealing with unruly students. Remind your troublemakers they can be arrested if necessary.

Our principal at high school graduation informed all students that sunglasses would not be permitted on the stage during formal ceremonies, as they were to receive their diploma with class. She added there were four police cars and officers just outside the arena nearby doors, who could be immediately called to deal with anyone who might seek to violate these rules and make a mockery of the graduation ceremony. The result was a dignified ceremony with full student compliance.

11. Have a Sense of Humor to Enliven the Learning Experience.

Everybody likes to have a good laugh. Laughter will diffuse much unwanted tension (both between the teacher and students, as well as between students). Laughter is a wonderful medicine that costs us nothing.

Beware of making fun of students, or encouraging such by students toward their peers. We want to uphold every individual. Good humor never degrades or belittles a person. Unfortunately however kids can be cruel and they rarely hold back.

Being also able to not take yourself too seriously as a teacher, apologize when you're wrong, and allowing yourself to have a laugh will endear your students to you.

To be any less in character is to be as the tin man in the Wizard of Oz. The educational system has enough teachers made of tin already, whose hearts have grown cold and their instruction become lifeless.

If your staff has become so rigid and frigid that they cannot laugh anymore, bring me in to encourage and uplift them. Principals, administrators, and senior teachers need to be willing to share their mess-ups and failures with new teachers.

We all have a bad day and fall short of our desirable expectation at times. To project otherwise will set your staff forever on edge and thereby make them too nervous to spontaneously teach using their gifts, talents, and abilities.

Administrators who project themselves as the pinnacle of perfection and doing everything by the book alienate new teachers (and some old ones too), while hindering their self-confidence and ability to teach at their highest level.

As a new teacher, when you leave the school at the end of your workday, find someone whom you can laugh with lest you lose it and go crazy.

Paul in Jamaica having a blast speaking at schools throughout Montego Bay, where children enthusiastically greeted him with smiles, laughter, and shouts of joy. The children were so excited and happy they tried to follow Paul as he left the school.

12. Be Sincere and Transparent

Sincerity is always appreciated more than sarcasm. Sarcasm, though humorous and fun at times, never draws people close to you to the extent sincerity will.

Students get enough sarcasm throughout the day from their peers. Within the classroom kids want to feel safe and assured as they participate in topical discussions.

Be sincere and transparent with your students. It takes time to earn students' trust. Little by little, step-by-step, as an educator you can endear your students to you and gradually gain their trust. Some students blindly give their trust to people in authority assuming and expecting the best outcome. Other students (perhaps those with parents who disappoint them and don't keep their promises) are a bit slow to put their trust in you.

Our principal gained respect from teachers for not withholding information she had gathered from the school board concerning upcoming budget cuts, layoffs, and changes. Likewise as a teacher give your students all of the information you can about upcoming events and initiatives concerning them.

Although your students may not understand everything fully, they will appreciate your honesty and sincerity. By being willing to tell students with transparency the latest goings on internally soon to affect them, they will grow to trust and respect you.

Keep in mind the age group you teach is of paramount importance when considering what information to tell. I taught high school students, who were mature enough to handle some things. Elementary or middle school students may not need to hear certain things.

Uphold the confidentiality due your school board, principal, administrators, and fellow teachers. Exercise caution in that what you tell kids, as they can distort, take things out of context, and emotionally react unnecessarily. Be wise and use discretion before unveiling information they can't handle.

Principals typically don't want teachers who won't be returning the next year to reveal such information to their students, lest students get mad at the principal or have their parents complain.

Therefore you have to be discerning as to what information is appropriate to share with your students and what is not. Let your heart be the judge and guide you.

Paul & Karla (his wife) comforting a distressed Snow White at the Orlando International Airport, a frequent point of departure for Paul's global travels and numerous speaking engagement throughout the world.

Invite Paul to speak in your city!

RevivingNations@yahoo.com

13. Share Your Academic Struggles and Successes.

Children greatly benefit from hearing about your personal struggles as a child. Struggles are something we all face during different times of our lives.

Sharing these struggles from your childhood and youth make kids feel normal and capable. When a child hears you tell a story of how you overcame something, it gives them hope that they too can overcome their personal struggles and challenges.

By referencing and talking about your small beginnings, it makes kids feel capable of overcoming obstacles and achieving greatness like you.

When I share my academic struggles, challenges, and pitfalls it helps students see our common bond. Opening up and sharing difficulties you have endured, persevered through, and triumphed over gives youth hope.

Whenever you are in the midst of a trying situation, often you have no feeling or desire within to go forward. Sometimes everything around you looks hopeless and causes the utmost despair within your heart.

Yet when you learn the art of walking by faith and not by sight, you can change your world and reverse the curse of the past. You can change your world by simply daring to do so.

If you wholeheartedly apply yourself, there is nothing you cannot do! Kids need to hear this repeatedly from you! Share the academic struggles and triumphs from your youth. Your stories will impart hope and strength within the hearts of your students to courageously conquer their present challenges.

Paul & Karla with Mickey Mouse at Walt Disney World in Orlando, Florida. One of Paul's claims to fame is when he, at the tender age of 17, worked at Disney World one summer.

Inside the Magic Kingdom Paul worked in Cinderella's Palace at King Stefan's Restaurant as a busboy in training to be a server. Although Paul never made it to be a server (as he quit the job to work as a lifeguard elsewhere), Paul did manage to date Cinderella while he was working for Mickey.

Nevertheless Paul thinks Karla is far more beautiful than a costume clad Cinderella and for this reason has made her is princess. Karla being from Canada was a miraculous catch and a God sent gift to Paul from afar. Karla is also an author and professional speaker like Paul. Her books on the environment, women's issues, home care, and money saving are incredible.

If you'd like Paul or Karla to speak in your city, don't hesitate to contact either of them at RevivingNations@yahoo.com

14. Recognize and Celebrate Student Successes

When one of my student's, a star soccer player, got front-page coverage on the sports page of our local newspaper, I read the entire article to the class.

Besides making my student feel really good, I further showed all of my students the importance of celebrating everyone's success.

By celebrating students' successes, we encourage students to do their best and excel in life. Success is contagious and must be celebrated to exponentially multiply.

Take ample time to recognize and celebrate your students' successes. Be hearty in your affirmation and lavish in your praise. As you do, it will send waves of love through the classroom and show your students you truly care about them.

Toward the end of the year when my teaching mentor began to put a simple smile at the end of her emails, it made me feel good. I actually began to see and feel her heart.

This simple act of humanity and kindness touched me. I therefore responded happily and thanked her for the smile. She thereafter continued for a while to conclude her emails with a smile. Then when my annual contract wasn't renewed (for whatever reason, which I didn't shed any tears over) she seemed to pull back and distance herself a bit.

It's a bit odd when administrators discontinue treating you like a person just because they know you won't be returning to work at their school the following year. This is something that must change internally among principals and administrators. Teachers are people who are not just to be used as tools and discarded when administrators are done with us.

My mom told me the State of Florida (unlike other states) doesn't even provide health insurance to its retired teachers. Such treatment of teachers who have given 30 years of their lives to serve in the public schools is unconscionable and shameful.

The county where I taught in Florida didn't provide full health insurance coverage when I was teaching. When I got a viral bacterial infection in my eye as a result of being around countless amounts of students, my school's health insurance only paid for about a third of the cost of my doctor's prescribed eye drops.

These are some of the small reasons educators don't return to work after teaching a few years. Most human beings and professionals prefer to go where they are celebrated not merely tolerated.

Your students are no different. Therefore treat them as human beings, not just pupils to be lorded over and told what to do. Show some heart and sympathy for your students.

Think back to when you were in school and had to study for multiple classes. It isn't always a fun and joyous experience. Therefore when a few small bright moments occur in a student's life, take time to celebrate with him or her.

Show some love! As you do, your students will undoubtedly love you back in return.

Turn your classroom into a place of affirmation and celebration. Make it such that kids want to be around you and grow in your presence.

15. Love and Recognize Your Students

During one teachers and staff meeting, our assistant principal (a wonderful man) suggested we just tell those students driving us crazy that we love them. He was kind of laughing when he said it, but it made sense (and certainly couldn't hurt) so I tried it.

Two students during the year who were disruptive and a bit annoying (an understatement), I had brief conversations with privately. Toward the end of the conversations with each young man, I told him: "I love you!"

Both of these young men at different times in the school year had gotten a bit verbally aggressive with me, giving me the evil eye and were deeply disrespectful to me in class. Nevertheless taking my assistant principal's advice, when I told the first of the challenging young men that I loved him, he replied, "I love you too!" The next thing I knew we were giving each other a hug and heartfelt smile.

Months later when the second young man and I had a conversation, he confided in me that he had been feeling down because of problems at home with his parents. When I phoned his parents the previous day, I noticed their phone had been disconnected. The young man also had eyes for an attractive young lady in the back of the room, who he was continually trying to persuade to go out with him.

By me just taking the time to listen to him for a few minutes and empathize with his current struggles, we immediately reconnected. He incidentally was one of my favorite students in his class, but he had a tendency to be a bit disruptive and occasionally rude.

Nevertheless when I told and affirmed my love for the young man, he immediately replied, "I love you too!"

That being said, always remember some of your biggest disciplinary problems often are looking for nothing more than attention. I was a bit of a clown and disciplinary problem myself in high school. At home I was quiet and introverted, not feeling comfortable around my stepmother. However in school I came alive and overcompensated for my quietness at home. Yet deep down I basically yearned for some love, attention, and affirmation.

Many times students feel like an emotional bottomless pit because their needs are not being met at home. Inwardly they are struggling and yearning for those vital needs to be met. Therefore as a teacher sometimes you have to be discerning and attentive to your students' emotional needs.

By pulling particular students aside sometimes, you can quietly speak to them and hear what is on their mind. As you do so, be open to listen to what they have to say. This way you can learn what is troubling them and adapt your disciplinary approach to connect with the student(s).

Otherwise you can be endlessly engaged in a power struggle that simply could be diffused and easily won by showing your students some heart and love.

Our school's computer network allows teachers to know students' birthdays, which is another wonderful way to add a personal touch to the classroom interaction. Be attentive to students' accomplishments, dreams, and interests. All of these are excellent ways to be human and show your students you genuinely care about them.

When one student brought a birthday cake to class, I allowed he and his classmates to have some to celebrate. By doing so, everybody was happy and appreciative. It didn't hurt their work productivity academically in the slightest. In fact it caused the students to apply themselves even more from the heart so as to please me and say thanks for allowing them to have a moment of celebration.

A little love and recognition goes a long way with your students. Being heartfelt and kind wins your students' respect.

16. Discover Students' Dreams and Build on Them!

When you take time to learn and discover students' dreams, you then as a teacher can build upon that foundation. The first assignment I give all of my students is to write an essay about their dreams and aspirations for the future.

As students begin to write and share with me their dreams for the future, we build an immediate bond and connection. I thereafter become their cheerleader for life, encouraging them every step of the way in route to dream fulfillment.

This way throughout the entire academic process, I can pinpoint their passion and propel their personal development by continually reminding them that these educational disciplines are vital to move them one step closer to dream fulfillment.

I therefore transcend the function of being merely their teacher for a single class and become their life coach who they can trust and count on throughout the duration of their life.

Instead of seeing yourself merely as an educator, see yourself also as a dream-maker. Cultivate an atmosphere in your classroom (and your life) that gives birth to dreams.

Many of my ESOL students who came from overseas have parents who struggle economically to survive. For these students their families often are happy just to be able to have a job that pays the bills and puts food on the table each month.

I know what that feels like because I have been there before. Yet to lift students and families up and out of that situation, we have to give birth to a paradigm shift within the thinking of people. To take students from the ghetto to get "mo" (more), we as teachers must inspire them to dream and then teach them how to daily pursue those dreams en route to their fulfillment.

Paul with youth from Bread of Life Chinese Church in Oviedo, Florida where he was the English / Young Adult Pastor for nearly three years. Today Paul's kids have all grown up and are excelling in college throughout the country. Others work for reputable companies or are entrepreneurs living their dreams.

Inspiring others to dream, boldly pursue their passion, and throw caution to the wind is a magnificent experience. To see the incredible results of those brave souls who dare to put feet to their faith is glorious and awe inspiring.

As educators we are given the opportunity daily to inspire young people, be the wind beneath their wings, and speak the words of encouragement they need to carry on when they are weary in well doing.

Therefore when you arise every morning, find ways to encourage your own heart so you can be fresh and impart words of inspiration to the students entrusted to your care.

17. Display Visuals For Your Students.

Visuals captivate and compel students to take immediate action en route to their destiny. Visuals awake students' imagination and internal imagery. As an English teacher in order to bring the language to life, visuals are a vital part of bridging the gap created by the language barrier.

Visuals also have a way of simply summarizing the main gist of the matter and lesson. Visuals help students get the main idea and the scope of the lesson.

There is a reason textbooks come with pictures. Seeing the word personified and described visually is often more memorable than merely reading the letters of the word.

Hence the age old adage which says, "A picture is worth a thousand words."

Consider living your life without pictures, images, and the ability to behold what is going on around you. Helen Keller was blind, but had extraordinary internal vision. As a teacher you need to awaken and evoke the imagination of your students.

Until you do, students will not come fully alive to the benefit of education. Once however you awaken the imagination within and empower students to creatively envision their dreams, you subconsciously become their best friend and empower them to be unstoppable en route to dream fulfillment.

Paul & Karla in lovely Sydney, Australia at the incredible Taronga Zoo with an adorable koala bear behind them. Australia is truly an amazing country full of beautiful beaches. Paul took his third visit to Sydney during his honeymoon with Karla, following a weeklong stay in Fiji. The two spent the second week of their honeymoon at the Shangri La Hotel overlooking Sydney Harbor and the famous Opera House.

18. Make Learning Fun!

Don't enter education with the old monotonous and boring paradigm that says teaching has to be dull. This mindset makes learning drudgery.

On the contrary, learning should be fun and full of meaningful exploration. Impart to your students the importance of the discovery process. Get students to realize the educational process and importance of their personal development beyond striving to just earn a good grade.

When you embrace personal development and commit to pursue personal growth, you will happily embrace education and make the grades you desire.

When students' hearts are right toward the benefits of education, the rigors of schoolwork will be embraced and not despised. It's hard to succeed at anything when you inwardly hate it.

Teachers therefore must excel at motivating students, not just barking at them to do their schoolwork. I'm often amazed at my students' attentiveness when I take five minutes to give them a pep talk and inspirational message.

I charge $350 an hour for a life coaching session (far more if I'm not feeling it or you annoy me), but my students often get it for free unbeknownst to them. I'm happy to awaken the giant within each of them. It's fun to see a holy hush come over them without me having to raise my voice.

When I speak from the heart, another depth of emotion and passion flows forth. This immediately and serendipitously arrests the hearts of my students, as they come into the grip of divine grace as my oratory gift explodes and engulfs the classroom.

There is an identifiable and notable difference from when I am teaching the county school board's assigned curriculum and inspiring my students from the heart. The difference is immediately discernable by my students. I can assure you, when the latter is in operation students are far more attentive.

One of my precious students, when hearing me speak passionately to my students from the heart, said: "Mr. Davis, you could be President." Another student said, "Mr. Davis, your face is getting red."

I laughed and said in Spanish, "Me gusta el fuego en mi corazon." This is my pitiful attempt at saying "I like the fire in my heart."

Truly there can be no pursuit or fulfillment of your destiny without some intensity. I try to match my students' level of intensity and passion in the classroom to captivate their hearts and inspire them to take action.

Sometimes it works and sometimes it doesn't, but we always have more fun when I put my heart into whatever we're doing. Teachers must know and always remember that even when you think students are not listening, they definitely are.

Often a quiet student is one who is internally processing what is being said. Quietness should not be mistaken for disinterest. Often it is quite the contrary, as the quiet student is mentally processing and taking in the stimuli at a very deep level so he or she can internalize and apply it to their lives.

19. Reward Academic Success and Good Behavior.

When a student excels in your class, find ways to reward them. Let them peer teach for extra credit. Permit them to sit wherever they want (if they aren't overly gregarious, otherwise that might not be the best idea). When they finish their assignment, allow them to read a book or magazine of their choice.

If the student seems interested in helping you, allow them to do some classroom tasks after they complete their work. Find ways to incorporate advanced students into your lesson planning and instruction. Otherwise I have found if you fail to draw advanced students in closer, allowing them to further participate and work with you as a teacher, they will become bored and be disruptive.

Slower learners need quiet and concentration. If your more advanced students get gregarious, this can greatly disrupt the students moving at a slower pace.

As an educator, you therefore must juggle the many different students' needs and provide a personal approach to everyone in the classroom. Make group assignments for all students, but then modify where necessary and accordingly for particular students needing a little bit more TLC (tender love and care).

Paul with Indonesian young men to whom he spoke at a drug rehabilitation facility in the island of Java. Afterward Paul took a trek with them into the lush green forest en route to this incredible waterfall, but not before having to hike over massive wet slippery rocks. Yet the dangerous rock climbing was well worth it when they reached this awesome waterfall.

The dedication of the businessman who founded this youth organization to help addicted children is notable. With nothing but faith (and no medical doctors assistance) he counsels and treats drug addicts, giving them nothing but unconditional love and a healthy lifestyle filled with a lot of exercise and outdoor activities to help them detox and rediscover the joy of living.

20. Encourage Student Teaching for Extra Credit

One of my student success stories was an ESOL student from Latin America named Hector. He immediately took a shine to me and was very diligent to always complete his assigned work.

Whenever I graded his essays, he would always take the time to rewrite his work to improve his writing skills. By doing so, he quickly mastered the use of the English language and the application of grammar techniques.

I was delighted when I heard that he won a county essay contest and received a laptop computer for his writing skills. He immediately came by to tell me and thank me for my contribution to his success.

It was one of those moments that made me feel as an educator that all of the hardship endured is worth it to see a student begin to succeed at this level.

Hector also was involved in peer teaching during class. Upon completing the class assignment, he would help me with other Latino students struggling to express themselves in English.

Peer teaching proved to be a priceless gem for me as an ESOL teacher, because I have a limited knowledge of Spanish. Furthermore English is a language that has more words than any other language on earth. That being said, translated vocabulary words from English to Spanish can be difficult if there is no such corresponding word in the language.

I learned this in Indonesia, a country where the language of Bahasa is so simplistic that it has no tenses. Bahasa has no past, present, or future tenses to its words. This makes for an easy language to learn, but a difficult language to translate complicated and sophisticated English to.

Peer teaching is a great way for teachers to involve students in the educational process, while at the same time further teaching by reason of reinforcement through repetition. Let's face it, you learn a subject far more when you teach it.

Merely studying a course to pass a test and meet a professional development requirement cannot compare to the extent you must master a subject to teach it. This is precisely why peer teaching is useful to students. Peer teaching further challenges advanced students to articulate and explain what they know, while helping slower and struggling students to hear an explanation of the lesson in the language of their peers.

Peer teaching provides a mutual win-win situation for everyone. Plus peer teaching further frees up teachers to take more time with each student, as educators walk throughout the room monitoring students' progress.

As we teach we also learn, often even more. Because to teach you have to first have a strong understanding of the material you are explaining. Providing students the opportunity to teach peers further solidifies and strengthens that which they know, while simultaneously helping struggling students move ahead academically.

You will be amazed at the discoveries advanced students make while they teach. Furthermore the light bulb of a struggling student's brain always responds better to helpful instruction from a peer than that of a teacher. I suppose it is a social thing and the level of comfort a student feels among his peers that makes it easier to learn from them.

21. Assign Meaningful and Thought Provoking Essays.

Unfortunately the American educational system has often been reduced to memorization rather than education. This is illustrated by the way tests are written by teachers.

Multiple-choice tests typically are the norm throughout the school system. Yet such test formats do not encourage critical thinking on the part of students.

Fill in the blank questions are better, but not much better because they too are all about memorization. The Socratic method of teaching, named after the Classical Greek philosopher Socrates, is a form of philosophical inquiry in which the questioner explores the implications of others' positions, to stimulate rational thinking and illuminate ideas

The Socratic method of teaching facilitates meaningful discussion, dialogue, and debate. Such is often quite foreign to the American educational system, where teachers drone on and like to hear their own voice. What we must remember however is that just because a teacher is talking does not ensure students are listening.

Students daydream as much as teachers talk. Therefore the way to get students actively engaged in the educational process is to facilitate meaningful classroom discussions through meaningful and stimulating questions, rigorous peer interaction (monitored by the teacher to ensure they stay on task), and written assignments (beyond the multiple guess scenario) where students are made to critically think.

Such might be a bit demanding for educators who don't think critically themselves. Not everybody naturally asks hard questions, examines things beneath the surface, and probes deeper. Hence the economic problems America and now the world are facing, by reason of blindly believing Wall Street and corporations who purported one thing publicly, while cooking the financial books privately.

Incidentally, my limited experience with administrators (who likely adhere to and closely conform to the dictates and directives of county school boards – their employer signing their paycheck) is that they prefer teachers who are quiet conformists rather than those who question and rock the boat.

I guess by now you know and can guess my personality type. You've got it! I like to rock, shake, and sometimes sink the boat! I'm sorry for being a bit of a troublemaker, but it is more fun!

As a teacher myself, I like to assign meaningful essays on topics that make students think. Intercepting students own personal lives and encouraging them to tell you their perspective based on their experience is powerful and enlightening both for students and teachers.

Some students excel more at classroom discussions, whereas other students tend to be a bit more shy and less inclined to speak up. Hence meaningful classroom discussions and essays are two means by which you can hear from all of your students.

I know for a fact a couple of my students were copying their peers' essays, instead of thinking and writing critically on their own. For example, one young man said he dreamed of shaking and moving his hips like Shakira. Based on his quiet personality and demeanor, I hardly gathered this was his true and deepest desire. Nevertheless what do I know? Maybe he wanted to break out of his quiet shell and master bodily movements on the dance floor. LOL

When I asked him if he had copied another young lady's work (a friend of his of the same nationality), he grinned and gave me a good smile as if to say he had been caught with his hand in the cookie jar.

Nevertheless even when students copy other students' essays, especially when they are ESOL students still becoming familiar with how to use the language, this is still advantageous and beneficial to their own learning. I don't encourage and tell my students this, but as an educator I know it to be true.

Moreover as a life coach, I can assure you students want (like everyone of us) to express their individuality and formulate ideas authentic to their personality. Eventually students will get frustrated and fed up with selling their soul to express someone else's ideas and dare to express their own.

I have seen this time and time again with my own ESOL students, who break out over time and begin to express themselves. It is a beautiful thing when an ESOL student from a foreign country drops their inhibition and begins to have fun with the English language.

I marvel in the choice of vocabulary my students throw out there in classroom discussions and their essays. I always try to salute and praise students for using new vocabulary rarely used by others.

One of my Colombian students (who had only been in the United States a couple months) used the word "dumbfounded" in an essay, which I congratulated him for giving him a high five in class.

Little fun ways of recognizing and congratulating students for stepping out with their use of language makes the learning process more enjoyable. It encourages more students to step out and dare to do the unordinary.

It is a shame and saddening to see students gripped by fear when they come to school. I like to liberate them and let them shine, as they trust and use their gifts, talents, and abilities.

I encourage risk taking as much as (if perhaps not more than) I exalt being right. When education is reduced to always being right, we've got something dead wrong. If it is all about just being right, we are putting our kids in a straightjacket and discouraging risk taking.

It was the educated risk takers like Edison, Einstein, Franklin, Bell, and Gates who pioneered new frontiers to alter the landscape of society. It is the risk takers who improve our quality of life and transform our world.

Imagine where we would be today had not Henry Ford and the Wright brothers dared to pursue their inventions and listened to the naysayer conformists.

Critical and creative thinking therefore needs to return to our classrooms. Part of educators job is not only teaching fundamentals and academic disciplines, but to inspire students' imagination. This is where we are missing the mark. It is time educators engineer some teaching techniques to birth some imagineering within students and encourage critical thinking to solve the problems of our present age. Otherwise another generation from overseas will be the next world leaders and we will be scratching our heads wondering what happened.

Paul & Karla sharing a romantic moment in Paris, France.

Paul in St. Augustine, Florida one of the nation's oldest and most historic cities. St. Augustine is one of Paul's favorite cities in Florida as it has both historic appeal and great beaches.

22. Be Your Own Cheerleader

Being an educator is often a thankless job. By the end of the day you sometimes feel overrun by administrators, exhausted from yelling at unruly kids, and overwhelmed with all of the papers to grade.

Being bulldozed by administrators and demanding county school board continuing education requirements can make even the most earnest new teachers think twice about staying in the educational profession.

Through it all there rarely is anybody to encourage you and tell you what a wonderful job you are doing. Often the focus is on what you are not doing, what you've not yet done, and what you need to do.

"Whew! Will it ever end?" That is certainly how I felt when I entered the lions' den.

After having some delightful experiences as a substitute teacher near my home, I thought teaching would be a cakewalk. Little did I know a rude awakening awaited me! Teaching and leaving at the end of the day is far easier than being a teacher on staff at a school, although the pay substantially differs.

Once employed as a teacher, the school and school board wants to own you. That means they want to assign continuing education, teachers' meetings, staff meetings, recruit you as a volunteer at night and during the weekends, and drop last minute surprises in your mailbox (including by email).

"Ah, ha! This is why my mom came home exhausted and feeling miserable after teaching everyday. Now I understand." I said to myself.

My mother taught for thirty years. My dad and I never could understand why she hated her job so much. We thought she had a great gig. After all, she had the summers and all major holidays off. She did not have to work during the weekends and she always got paid each month.

Little did we know the daily ordeal, she had to endure every time she went to school to teach. How ironic it is that adults return to school to teach, after enduring it for so many years as a kid growing up!

Obviously there is a reality check that abruptly comes at some point during an educator's career, when they realize this is not what they signed up for. Teachers enter the profession thinking they will be teaching eager and desirous kids who genuinely want to learn. (This was more my experience teaching English in Taiwan, as Asian students are more respectful and desirous of learning.)

I also taught international students at Aspect Language Institute in Orlando, Florida. This teaching scenario was also a wonderful experience because it consisted more of teaching than administrative work. My students were the best and the brightest from Latin America, Asia, and the Middle East.

These youth had come to America at a great expense to their parents (many governors, doctors, lawyers, mayors, politicians, etc. in their respective countries), as the annual tuition was around $16,000 at the time. Some came to have a bit of a vacation in the United States. Undoubtedly there were some mixed motives as to why they came, but nevertheless they remained respectful in class and were quick to try to learn the language.

There were far less disciplinary problems and power struggles with these students compared to my students in the public school. This also proved to be true in Europe, where I taught European students English. They genuinely wanted to be there and it was a pleasant experience.

The public school scenario is more obligatory for youth living in America. Therefore as teachers we somehow have to reframe the way students see it to lessen their resistance and daily rebellion to the educational process. We have to make students see how education is advantageous, while sympathizing with them that we realize often attending school is a choice made for them by their parents.

Yet if we can persuade students that going to school is for their own good and personal advancement, we will be more likely to see students willingly embrace education from the heart.

As teachers navigating through this arduous process, we must become our own cheerleaders. Considering the initial resistance sometimes of students, if we are not careful we can be made to feel like we are kids' enemies and allow ourselves to subconsciously be demonized (and thereby dehumanized) by them.

We therefore need to remember (and continually remind ourselves) that we are the good guys and potentially our students' very best friends. Because if students fail to get a good education, their lives can be extremely hard after they leave the confines of the classroom and enter the cruel real world.

It is necessary that teachers subtly and cleverly (best if done covertly without the students thinking you are doing this) challenge the misnomers and stereotypes about teachers. By doing so and reforming students' beliefs about educators, teachers can regain and earn the rightful respect of students. Respect is earned (not blindly given), not demanded. Yet by leveling and talking straight to kids, they can see things more clearly and thereby become more cooperative.

Apart from all of this, educators need to encourage themselves continually and keep some thick skin to endure the many blows that will come their way throughout the day.

When I say blows, I mean blows to your ego. Unruly and foul students can be very degrading of teachers. This can cause a teacher great embarrassment. Yet if you stay cool and don't take yourself too seriously, you can transcend the bumps in the road en route to achieving teacher success.

In your own heart, highlight your daily successes. Focus on your accomplishments and achievements with your star students and the struggling students who you've been able to help. Even if there is just one student in all of your classes who inspires you, focus on that student (not at the expense of all the other students) within your own heart to motivate you onward.

As you build on the success you've had with other students, those successes will begin to build your confidence and be transmitted in your dealings with other students. Success is contagious. Therefore focus on what you are doing right in your classes and student successes. As you do, you will fine turn your teaching approach and methodology to more easily impact a greater number of students.

By being your own cheerleader, you will avoid and overcome the many internal battles that overwhelm and undo many wonderful teachers.

Find ways to encourage yourself. Preserve your energy and guard your heart. Predetermine the best way to spend your time during your planning period and lunch. Beware of educational leeches, peers in the teaching profession who just want to gossip and suck the life out of you.

Being your own cheerleader means you surround yourself with positive people and eliminate the negative.

Paul at Mt. Bromo in the island of Java, Indonesia celebrating after a long trek up and around a volcano, which he saw erupt at sunrise. Indonesia is one of Paul's favorite places on earth!

One of Paul's dreams is to touch every nation on earth, while traveling around the world inspiring and empowering people to live their dreams. Help Paul fulfill his goal by supporting his IRS approved nonprofit organization Dream-Maker Ministries.

Dream-Maker Ministries
PO Box 684, Goldenrod, FL 32733 USA

Donations are also welcome through paypal.com at
RevivingNations@yahoo.com

Paul welcomes speaking invitations throughout the world, even in war-torn and third world countries where few dare to go! With your partnership and support together we can make a difference in our world and enrich the next generation!

23. Don't Let Others Demonize You

Not letting others demonize you does not mean you have to stand up and defend yourself. On the contrary, remain quiet outwardly, but inwardly don't internalize what those who demonize you may say about you.

Remember the truth always outlives a lie. Let your work product, heartfelt efforts, and success with your students speak for itself.

Crabby teachers who seek to gossip and pull others down are a waste of your time. Stay away from them, lest you be pulled into their toxic web.

Daily affirm yourself with wholesome words and self talk. Never allow outsiders to put their map on you, size you up, and diminish who you are as a person.

Beyond your profession, you are a person. Your individuality and personhood eclipses what you do professionally. Although your coworkers may not see it that way and may not know you intimately, don't feel obligated to stick up for yourself and make your thoughts known.

Often asserting yourself just further muddies the water and sets the stage for you to drown in it. Settle it in your heart that people will always gossip and that there is nothing you can do about it, other than control your response and attitude.

When you die, people will talk about how they embalmed you and the makeup job on your face (if you have an open casket funeral and a viewing – certainly not my cup of tea). Therefore get over it! Live your life free from the defilement of others' conversations about you.

Be your own cheerleader and show yourself unconditional love.

As you do, people who in the past gossiped and spoke evil about you, will be brought to not. Your lifestyle will always and eventually prove to be louder than the noise of a negative person.

Negative folks eventually get found out and exposed for what they are. People eventually catch on and see the true colors of a gossip queen – not an endearing quality by any means.

Therefore you predetermine and purpose in your own heart to be an up person no matter how down the world may be around you.

The sun always shines above the clouds. So you decide daily to keep your head up and remain focused on the stars. As the light of your countenance rises, you will live above the futile chatter of others and surpass their shallow stream of negativity.

Cream always rises to the top. Just be confident, settled, and secure. Lifelong consistency and longevity is the best cure for a critic's stupidity.

Just go to class, teach your kids, and keep on doing your thing. In due time you shall rejoice and sing as your adversaries are found out and judged for the harm they've caused you (and likely others).

Give yourself a pep talk everyday and remain happy along the way. Remember some of your students from dysfunctional families may be coming to school to see your smile, perhaps the only smile they will see today. Don't disappoint them. Smile! If necessary, fake it until you make it!

24. Avoid Gossip and Unwholesome Talk

Nobody likes to hear or listen to someone complain. Do yourself a favor and bite your lip before you entertain disdain for another human being. Remember only God above knows another person's heart and when you judge, you often are wrong or too harsh because you don't know the full story of their life.

Perhaps someone may be struggling on his or her job. Before you speak evil of them consider their other life challenges. Maybe their spouse is cheating on them, or abusing them at home. Maybe their child just died. Maybe they are caring for their sick elderly mother. Maybe their sibling is dying of cancer. Maybe they are thinking of quitting the job anyhow because it is not a good fit for them.

The possibilities are endless. Resist the urge to denigrate and speculate. You never fully know what a person may be dealing with in their life. The unknowns are endless. Therefore have some compassion and understanding before you jump to conclusions.

Unfortunately, it seems in the educational profession (as in many other lines of work) the only exercise some people get is jumping to conclusions. Nevertheless you can separate yourself quickly from the rest by being an upstanding individual who upholds everybody giving them the benefit of the doubt.

25. Don't Dump Your Problems on Your Students.

Don't confide in, nor dump your problems on your students. Find a safe place outside of the your school to let down your guard and be real. Get somebody off your campus to go to and vent when necessary.

Find a friend, family member, spouse, or a shrink outside of your place of work. This will sustain and protect your professionalism on the job, while ensuring you maintain proper respect with your students.

Remember familiarity will breed contempt. Beware who you show cracks in your armor to. Don't forget kids are cruel. Think back to when you were in school and all of the nasty jokes that were said. Even friends rag on each other in school. What makes you think as an educator a student wouldn't turn on you in a moment's notice when it is advantageous to them?

Don't throw yourself under the bus by reason of confiding in the wrong people. Besides your students do not have the level of maturity (intellectually and emotionally) to be able to advise or sympathize with you.

Paul with his buddy Eugene at New Smyrna Beach, FL.

26. Live a Balanced Life.

Beware of getting so consumed and involved in work at your school that your social life revolves around everything on campus. When you give out to that extent at school and eliminate your social life elsewhere, you open yourself up emotionally to get hurt and offended when your expectations are not met.

Singles who are lonely (or married individuals who feel neglected by their spouse) are prime candidates to becoming overly emotionally attached to their school. Don't get me wrong I think you should have an emotional attachment to where you work. How else could you be passionate and purposeful about your profession without an emotional connection?

What is cause for concern however is becoming (or already being when entering the teaching profession) an emotional bottomless pit. If you are emotionally needy, working for a school (particularly a high-school or college) can be a great place to cultivate meaningful relationships at work and during extracurricular activities.

Yet this should not be your chief aim and objective. To go into the teaching profession (or volunteer for school functions) with this mixed motivation, can result in unwanted controversy and conflict in the event someone you pursue relationally shows no interest and does not reciprocate.

That being said as a rule of thumb it is always good to separate your work and personal life, lest the latter (or pursuit thereof) jeopardize your professionalism.

Living a balanced life means you care for yourself physically, emotionally, intellectually, socially, and spiritually. However that may be, you in your own unique way attend to each of these vital aspects of your personal wellbeing.

Exercise is important to remain physically healthy and perform your job at peak performance. When energy levels drop, everything in your day beginning with your focus and productivity will plummet.

Getting a proper amount of sleep, not burning the candle at both ends, and eliminating unwanted sources of stress from your life all will keep you happy and healthy. Don't be afraid to erect healthy perimeters around your life. Structure your life to minimize annoyances and irritants.

Answer machines, voice mail, caller ID, and modern technology are to be used for your convenience to enhance your life. Never feel obligated to answer phone calls and emails of no interest to you. If it doesn't add to and enhance your life, refuse to attend to it.

Robbing yourself of 7 to 8 hours of sleep daily is the first thing that prematurely ages your body. Secondly, stress is a major source of fatigue, which will wear and tear your body down rapidly.

Therefore honor and schedule proper time to sleep every night. Don't ever feel obligated to be superman or superwoman. Know your limitations and bodily needs. Never feel guilty for saying no to preserve your health.

Remember nobody cares about your body as much as you. Therefore eat healthy and regulate your intake of sweets and fatty foods. Minimize sugar and salt consumption, which causes you to retain water and become bloated.

Eat plenty of fiber daily (through fiber rich cereals, multi-grain bars, fruits, nuts, and vegetables). A sufficient amount of fiber will keep you regular, while enabling your body to eliminate that which is no longer needed in your body.

Unfortunately, Americans intake and assimilate daily more than we eliminate by way of food consumption. Hence we are growing wider daily and are now known as the most obese nation on earth. Fat and sassy, we are arrogant and haughty. Despite our phenomenal medical breakthroughs, it is we who are now dying prematurely because of our inability to eat healthy and regulate our caloric consumption daily.

A balanced life consists of moderation, regulation, and making wise choices when it comes to consumption. Success is determined by what you say no to. Saying no to driving after having a few adult beverages is a great place to start.

Poor decisions in a moment's notice can cut short your life. Alcohol also slows down your metabolism's ability to burn fat, not to mention it kills brain cells. Therefore if you drink, do so in moderation.

Living a balanced life means you remember your job is not your life. Take time for yourself, family, and friends. Do what you love rather than being constrained by what you dislike. Break out and live your life your way without apology.

Although you teach, take some time for pleasurable reading when you feel like it. If you have no interest in picking up a book after teaching all week, than don't. Get out and enjoy the beauty of creation and nature.

Be free and be yourself. Remember you are only bound to your job description. Any other additional ambiguities not written explicitly in your contract are not obligatory, nor mandatory. Only help out beyond your job description when you truly desire to do so from the heart.

What good is it to give of yourself and do well, if inside you are bitter and angry about it? Eventually such bitterness will surface and defile many. It is far better to be committed to your school in heart, even though you sometimes (or often if you must depending upon your personal demands and restrictions) have to say no to requests for additional help beyond your job, than to be burnt out because of endless requests you have no desire to fulfill.

Paul & Karla in lovely Monte Carlo along the gorgeous Mediterranean just before the famous Grand Prix. Ferraris, yachts, picturesque beaches, fabulous cuisine, and enchanting architecture! Life in Monaco is magical. We like staying in nearby Nice, France and driving to Monte Carlo with the breathtaking views and phenomenal smell of jasmine in the air.

If you need a quick travel visa to be carefree and footloose:
http://click.linksynergy.com/fs-bin/click?id=3RWH2TJD1YU&offerid=149854.10000004&type=3&subid=0

If you don't have a passport, fear not! Get one in 24 hours:
http://click.linksynergy.com/fs-bin/click?id=3RWH2TJD1YU&offerid=140795.10000018&type=3&subid=0

For great airfare, hotel deals and travel insurance:
http://click.linksynergy.com/fs-bin/click?id=3RWH2TJD1YU&offerid=163957.10000008&type=4&subid=0

27. Don't Feel Guilty About Not Being Able to Help

Our lives consist of time, which is our most precious resource. Therefore guard and treasure time more than your money. Finances can be replaced, but not time. When time is gone, it is gone forever.

Few educators on their deathbed wish they had given more time to their school. Many however regret giving so much of themselves that they never fully enjoyed their lives.

You therefore should never feel guilty for taking back your life and spending it according to the desires of your heart. You don't have to wait until you are sixty or seventy years old to have permission to enjoy your life.

Go on a vacation whenever you want and enjoy it! If you must, keep your personal vacations to yourself lest other teachers around you become jealous. Share with those who genuinely care, but as for the others who make you feel uncomfortable and guilty for living your dreams don't share your precious jewels with them.

Paul speaking in Brasilia, the capital of Brazil, to a crowd of 50,000 people during a citywide celebration.

Paul in Pakistan praying with a Muslim man and his wife who was barren and wanting to get pregnant to bear a child.

Truly there are so many precious people in the world and an enormous amount of needs that we all have. You as one individual can only do so much. Therefore pinpoint your passion, discover your purpose, cooperate with your Creator, and live your dreams in accordance with divine design.

Cultivate contentment inwardly and never feel guilty for that which you cannot do. Be thankful and attentive to that which you can (and inwardly desire to) do.

Herein you shall find contentment and great success.

28. Learn from Other Sincere and Helpful Teachers

Every school has some sweet and sincere teachers who are happy to befriend and help you. Thankfully for me, that proved to be my senior ESOL teacher with five years experience under her belt.

Whether she was genuinely desirous to help me or bound by reason of her job description and duty, I don't know. However I would like to think so.

I know my questions and requests for help did not always come at the ideal time. Nevertheless I tried to keep my questions and requests for help to a minimum, while practicing brevity and valuing my superior's time.

Check around your school and get to know other veteran teachers who are upbeat. These souls are seasoned and established in their professions. If they don't hate their job already, they probably will be happy to help you if you were to ask. Take the initiative and ask for help whenever you need it.

One ESE (Exceptional Student Education) teacher helped me out with an online course when I was a bit behind. It only took about a minute to answer my question and get me moving in the right direction, but had he or somebody else not helped me I might have never done the assignment altogether.

When I say help, sometimes it isn't all that big of a request. Yet if it is important to please administration, fulfill your requirements, and complete the necessary tasks within your job description than it is needful.

Getting done that which is necessary as a new teacher will sometimes be a daunting task. Don't hesitate or be shy to ask for help when you need it. On the other hand, lend a helping hand when you can to other teachers in need. Your good name will then go before you and open the way for you to receive help when you need it.

Paul in Mozambique, Africa traveling by river between countries. It was so hot Paul wanted to jump in the river to cool off, but the locals forbid him saying there were deadly crocodiles waiting below to eat whatever entered the water.

Apparently many animals, children, and women who come to the river to wash their clothes are easy prey for vicious crocodiles hiding below until the opportune time to attack.

Thankfully the natives know the terrain and the impediments to thwart any trip in Africa. Likewise as an educator we new teachers need to listen to the aged and veteran teachers among us who possess wisdom and skill to guide us along.

29. Don't Disrespect the School Structure and Policies.

The department of education within each state across the nation has its own guidelines and federal mandates that it is endeavoring to adhere to. Some states have additional guidelines and procedures they follow. Policies across the school boards within each state may also differ.

Before you get all worked up emotionally over things beyond your control, realize what you can and cannot change. Not everything is open for discussion. You therefore as an educator need to humbly accept some things and submit to the authority of the school board presiding over you.

Professional teacher unions are a good place to explore advocating new legislation and lobbying for change in your state.

Paul at the tsunami epicenter in Banda Aceh, Indonesia.

Paul with his police & security entourage when speaking in Pakistan after 9-11 on peace, reconciliation, and global cooperation between nations.

A British schoolmaster told Paul teachers in his private school along with hired help of Pakistani origin were murdered at school when young terrorists gunned down security guarding the entrance and killed school workers. Elsewhere a moderate Muslim newspaper was bombed for printing an article saying you don't have to have a long beard to be a good Muslim. Paul therefore spoke on peace, tolerance and reconciliation; reminding religious groups God is a life giver not a killer.

Overcoming terrorism without addressing the religious element and cross-cultural stereotypes is futile. Paul however dived into these issues without hesitation when speaking in this historically volatile region. The demonization of nations and people will only stop when we cease to think of ourselves as superior. Nothing is more evil than deeming others to be inferior to us, while we pontificate our own goodness.

Self-righteousness is never kosher in the eyes of the world.

http://click.linksynergy.com/fs-bin/click?id=3RWH2TJD1YU&offerid=143177.10000116&type=3&subid=0

30. Invest in Your Professional Development & Personal Happiness.

Beyond continuing education to satisfy the requirements of your county school board, consider pursuing classes in topics of interest to you. Be a lifelong learner, not because you have to but because you want to.

When you are a student yourself in some small capacity, it keeps you inquisitive and curious. Being a student yourself enables you to always stay fresh and self-aware as an educator as to how your students feel.

Being stretched academically is never easy. By being stretched a bit yourself, you maintain a tender heart and cultivate compassion for your students. This will bring out the cheerleader and exhorter in you within the classroom.

As you relate stories about your own professional development, your students will feel more deeply connected to you rather than assuming you are aloof to their struggles.

Travel internationally to experience another culture, country, and people. Embrace things foreign so you can be more traveled and experientially wise as an educator. Schools across the country are becoming increasingly diverse with international students.

My world travels make for great stories and instructional pieces whenever I am teaching. Students across the world having immigrated to Florida love to hear that their teacher has been to their home country. It immediately creates a deeper bond between a teacher and students.

Find ways to invest in your own personal happiness. By cultivating happiness in your own life, you will arrive to the classroom fresh and full of life for your students. The last thing students' need is another grumpy teacher to make them miserable.

Many community colleges have EPI programs, which stands for *Educator Professional Institute*. These are very accommodating programs as many teachers currently employed take classes during the evenings to fulfill state requirements.

Troops to Teachers is a wonderful resource for military personnel seeking to transition into teaching. I also found an online Masters degree in Educational Leadership offered by the University of West Florida (UWF), located in the Florida panhandle, should anyone be desirous of pursuing working within administration at schools. A link to get you started is http://onlinecampus.uwf.edu/offer/grad.cfm#ETMS.

The administration and management online program at UWF was voted the "best buy" for 2009 by www.GetEducated.com. For more information about the Masters degree program in Educational Leadership contact Dr. Karen Rasmussen at krasmuss@uwf.edu or phone 850-474-2301. Military service personnel may contact a UWF advisor at MilitaryAdvisor@uwf.edu.

When you write or phone tell them Paul Davis, author of "New Teacher Success & Survival Secrets" told you about their program ...to ensure you get the red carpet treatment.

For those of you moving into teaching from other professions, you will need to take several exams to obtain your teacher certification. I found the New York Department of Education (at the writing of this book) has free downloadable study guides for teachers preparing to test on any given subject.

The Florida Department of Education charges (at the writing of this book) approximately $5.62 per study guide for any given subject a prospective teacher wants to prepare for their test. As for me I took and passed the English 6-12 and ESOL exams, along with all of the general knowledge and professional exam.

Among the study guides I used beyond those provided by various state departments of education, are those below which I found helpful to adequately prepare me for testing.

XAMonline.com – Teacher Certification Specialists

Passthetexes.com – Test Prep for the ESL exam

My methodology for studying for these various exams was simply to go to the answer key of these books, get all of the correct answers, understand the reasoning, and then memorize what the Florida Department of Education wants me to know. The books and various study guides definitely helped me. Mention Paul and "New Teacher Success & Survival Secrets" to ensure you get the preferential treatment and latest books.

Paul & Karla at the Golden Gate bridge in exquisitely beautiful San Francisco, California near the Presidio where Paul's maternal grandparents lived while his grandfather (a retired U.S. Army Lt. Colonel) was stationed for a season during his military years of service.

Paul at Carmel Beach in California with friends following a youth conference in San Jose, where Paul spoke that week.

Carmel Beach is very unique and unusual in that the temperature is significantly cooler than San Francisco, just a short drive away. Moreover Carmel Beach is also home to many famous art galleries and museums. It was a joy to visit and experience. There are truly many wonderful places throughout California, which makes it one of Paul's favorite states.

Paul lived in Orange County, southern California for two-and-a-half years while attending Bible College. Laguna Beach and Irvine are two of Paul's favorite places in Orange County. During his days at college, Paul worked part-time at Mimi's Café (a phenomenal French restaurant, which since has branched out and opened locations in Central Florida much to Paul's delight). Among Paul's other part-time employment ventures in Irvine was working as a lifeguard at Wild Rivers and a personal fitness trainer at 24 Hour Fitness at UCI.

The Irvine Hyatt also employed Paul as a doorman for a bit just before he went overseas to live in Southeast Asia, where he traveled throughout ten nations speaking and ministering.

Small sacrifices truly can lead to big blessings,
when we pay the price to intelligently invest in ourselves.

31. Be a Lifelong Learner.

It's amazing how many educators are stagnant in their own learning and professional development. Being a lifelong learner however is invigorating and exciting.

There are limitless bodies of knowledge we all can pursue and learn. Acquiring knowledge and learning new things is fun! My wife Karla is always diving into a new body of knowledge pertaining to health and the environment. Her book *Green Home Guide* is a phenomenal read about how to save money, protect your family, and preserve your health.

Like my father I made sure when I went looking for a wife that I found a beautiful and an intelligent woman. Karla is precisely that, providing me both beauty to behold and intellectual stimulation to enliven my mind.

When I began teaching I was shocked to hear the foul language being used by high-school students. Everyday I walked from my classroom to the cafeteria I would hear grotesque and vile language being spit out by kids. What troubled me even more was the lack of regard for administrators and teachers as we passed by them. They had no shame, nor hesitation to speak in such a way. This told me that such manner of speech was sadly becoming acceptable socially, both by families and in the educational system.

As I contemplated on ways to confront this national problem and epidemic of foul language dumbing down our young minds and decaying our moral fiber, I immediately thought of my wife Karla's book *Classy Woman* to empower women to be elegant and influential in society.

When we learn proactively and purposefully, learning occurs with energy and vitality. Likewise no student enjoys learning something he or she deems irrelevant. That is why educators must build on students' daily life experiences, identify their dreams, and build a foundation for desirable learning.

As a lifelong learner, avoid professors at colleges and universities who irritate you. I recall being enrolled in an EPI class at a local community college, which usually is excellent and always a wonderful experience. In fact I earned my Associate in Arts degree from this same college before transferring to UCF, where I went on to earn my Bachelors degree.

The professor presiding over one of the EPI classes I was enrolled didn't impress me the first day of class. She was complaining about her computer and showing an extreme level of impatience.

Considering computers and operating systems within academia typically take me a while to learn, I immediately felt this professor was not one I wanted to take a class with at this time in my life. I was recovering from a car accident, fighting my insurance company, learning a new operating system at school where I was teaching, and acclimating to all of the many demands of being a new teacher. Plus I was already enrolled in one other evening class at the same college.

Trusting my instincts, I immediately dropped the class the next day. When the college said I dropped the course a day late (after the period of time wherein a refund could be granted) and could not receive a refund, I wrote a letter to the college president stating the above information and that it was unfair to not permit students to withdraw from a class until they first meet their teacher on the first day. Thankfully, the college kindly refunded me my tuition for the cost of the class.

As long as learning remains fun, you will happily embrace being a lifelong learner. This has always been my objective. My home library is about as large as the school library, where I taught as a first year teacher.

Millionaires invest in books and getting to know intelligent people. TVs and entertainment systems are not as important to them as growing personally and investing in their professional development. When educators embrace the same mentality, teachers will be better able to facilitate meaningful conversations within the classroom and actively engage their students at every level.

Paul exploring majestic Mt. Bromo and adjacent active volcanoes erupting in the distance in the island of Java, Indonesia. This was an incredible early morning trek uphill in chilly temperatures, but well worth it at sunrise to see this incredible sight – a first for Paul.

Paul at the New York Modern Museum of Art doing a double take at this artistic design. Truly things are not always as we first think they appear.

Undoubtedly life offers us many illusions. Teaching is no different as what we expect often turns out differently and is cause for us to reevaluate our approach. Yet the rigors and demands of teaching always afford us many opportunities for personal and professional growth.

Sometimes in life when you get what you want, you no longer want what you've got. It is during these times you must reevaluate, reexamine your pursuits, reposition in alignment with your purpose, and regain your focus.

32. Wholeheartedly Praise Students!

Nothing feels better than being praised by your teacher in front of your peers in class. Students love to be recognized for being brilliant in the presence of their classmates.

When students make the effort, participate in class, and consistently do their homework; we as educators owe it to them to praise their hard work and heartfelt efforts.

Unfortunately this is something many educators fail to do as they get caught up in the daily grind, following the curriculum, and staying on task. In all of our teaching, lecturing, and classroom preparation we must never forget to treat our students like human beings.

It is so easy to focus on the few unruly and disruptive students, that we forget to honor and encourage the good students who daily do what is asked of them. Let us not be so eager to harness the mischievous troublemakers in class that we forget to honor and praise our little angels who do as they are told.

Not all students will earn A's and B's in your class, but if they give a heartfelt effort and consistently do what is expected of them, it is only fair and right for you to praise them. Sadly, this type of praise and encouragement is not measured out enough for the average student.

As an ESOL teacher, I love to praise my students who give a good effort at mastering new vocabulary, participating in class discussions, and writing essays in an unfamiliar language.

One student who just arrived from Colombia knew hardly any words in English. Nevertheless he was put in my 11th and 12th grade English class.

Imagine if you went to China, knowing only a few words and were put into a high-school class taught in Mandarin (the language of China). How would you feel?

Often we forget to put ourselves in our students' shoes and consider how they feel. If we were to do so more often, our teaching and instruction would have far more heart and patient understanding.

Unfortunately, the tendency among teachers is to become the drill sergeant or harsh taskmaster, continually barking out the next order. Is it any wonder students eventually feel overwhelmed and can't take it any more?

Students want to be taught by a human being, not a dictator. If a student cannot see your humanity and feel your heart, it is unlikely he or she will cooperate and learn to the full extent of their potential. Students hold back their full power and passion when they don't like or trust their teacher.

When we buy a house or a car, we as educators like to work with sales agents or reps we know, like and trust. Yet when we teach school, we often forget to show ourselves to be likeable. We often feel so intimidated and dominated by administration breathing over our necks to comply with all of the state and school board mandates that we resort to dehumanizing the educational experience for our students in exchange for rigid compliance to all that is expected of us as educators. And who suffers the most? Our students.

By tenderly and happily cultivating my new Colombian student named Pacho, I suddenly saw him step out and begin using the language. I praised Pacho wholeheartedly for his clever use of the language and application of new words rarely used by other students.

Although Pacho was previously a continual disciplinary problem for me, he came alive by reason of me being patient and praising him consistently. It wasn't long before Pacho was doing his assignments and surprising us all.

Truly, leaving your country (often against your will to obey and accompany your parents to the United States) and your friends behind is not easy. I had a firsthand glimpse into the lives of these students who immigrate to a new country and suddenly are told to learn a new language (and be schooled entirely academically in that new language). It is nothing less than a double whammy that can be socially and intellectually devastating for many young people.

As an ESOL teacher, I therefore need to be an understanding friend and cheerleader as much (if not more) than an educator. By doing so, I can give students immigrating hope that at least there is one class in school they have a cheerleader who cares about them and won't heartlessly fail them (without considering their life challenges).

I remember when Salvador arrived the first day in my class and was scared out of his wits when I asked him to read a paragraph during a read along exercise. He hardly spoke much English, although he was well liked by his classmates.

Salvador's gentle nature and warm smile endeared us all. Hence I tried a more gentle approach as his teacher to gradually warm him up to the language. Little by little, step by step, high five by high five, joking and smiling with him everyday; I managed to chip away at the wall of fear until it eventually fell down and Salvador playfully sought to speak in English.

I shall never forget the first time Salvador dared to give it a go and participate in a read along in class. We all applauded (and I nearly cried) after Salvador finished reading his first paragraph in English. I met him afterward at his desk to give him a high-five. "Excellente!" I said to Salvador in Spanish.

He smiled warmly with great pride at his accomplishment and ability to use the new language. From that day onward, Salvador never hesitated to read a few sentences during read along exercises in class. I later would use Salvador as a testimonial and motivator to other new students who would arrive from afar full of fear.

Little by little as I adapted my approach to each student, treating them all as unique and precious souls, the walls came down and the language began to be spoken with childlike joy. Making learning fun and uplifting everyone always works for me as an educator. It may take longer with some students than others, but as you love them unconditionally and praise them wholeheartedly, eventually you shall see the transformation occur suddenly.

There can be no greater reward for an educator than to see transformation within your students and an attitude adjustment as learning is happily embraced.

Karla & Paul with his parents' dog Ginger enjoying a day with the family in sunny Florida. Ginger was a stray dog Paul's mom rescued alongside the street. Ginger was a bit shy and scared at first, but has become the sweetest and perfect family pet.

Save on your pet meds and don't overpay.
http://click.linksynergy.com/fs-bin/click?id=3RWH2TJD1YU&offerid=56753.10000185&type=4&subid=0

33. Honor and Uphold All Students

Like any teacher, we all have our favorites. Yet it is vital to uphold and honor all of your students, even those who try your every last nerve.

Upholding the dignity of every student (and your fellow teachers and administrative staff) is important to your professional success as an educator. I recall one of my students who had an unusual body odor (which smelled like old Chinese food ready to be thrown out).

The students nearby him in class began to make fun of him. Incidentally, the student sat directly next to me. My first year of teaching was such that I did not have a very large classroom for my nearly fifty ESOL students who I taught throughout the day. My class sizes thankfully were usually no more than twenty-two students per class.

Half of my classes consisted of twelve or less students, which was perfect for me as a new teacher. Considering all of the various levels among my learners, I had to somewhat tailor make instruction for each student based on where they were in their learning of the English language.

Yet when I wasn't given my own desk as a teacher and was made to share the tables with my students, I knew it was going to be an interesting year. Thankfully the close proximity with my students didn't drive me crazy. My students were surprisingly respectful and a joy to teach.

Don't misunderstand me. We had our moments and trying times. Certainly sitting next to a student with bad body odor was no delight first thing in the morning. Having your stomach turn and feeling nausea immediately when you begin your workday is not pleasant. When it is due to something (or someone) beyond your control, it can make you feel a bit powerless.

Thankfully the students gave the young man some subtle (and not so subtle) hints that he needed to bathe. I don't know if his family was struggling financially, but I thought such might be the case. I speculated to myself that perhaps he wasn't washing his clothes.

I had recalled him saying he lived with his father and didn't remember hearing anything about a mother being at home with him. Therefore I tried to be extremely merciful and as understanding as possible. Yet the smell was a bit of a distraction both for me and the other students.

In such instances of possible neglect (even though he was a high-school student able to wash his own clothes ...assuming his parents provide him the washing machine, detergent and electricity) I make a referral to the guidance counselor to see if there is any way they can privately and quietly intervene.

I guess the rude remarks by his classmates eventually were sufficient motivation to get the young man to bathe and care for himself properly, because thankfully the body odor went away. During this time however I really had to hold my tongue and consciously make an effort to uphold the dignity of this student.

I reminded my class that our identity is not found in that which we wear or necessarily do, but in who we are as a person. I told my students of my own struggles when my father and stepmother gained custody of me. When I left the comfort and care of my maternal grandparents, I moved into a doublewide trailer with my parents. We were obviously struggling economically and I could feel the pinch immediately.

I hardly felt comfortable asking for money to get a haircut or clothes for school. In fact my grandparents often had to intervene to ensure I had such necessities. Those days in which I was in middle school were very challenging for me. Many of my classmates had stylish clothes and pocket money to have fun at any given whim. Not so for me.

By relating my personal struggles, my students began to realize that the majority of what they have (that they think makes them cool and respectable in the eyes of their peers) comes from the generosity of their parents.

I therefore reminded my students that we should not look down on another student who doesn't have such niceties because after all these things usually come from parents caring for them. Nobody should be made to feel inferior just because their parents cannot provide all of the latest fashionable clothing and technological gadgets seen as status symbols by youth.

Graciously my students embraced the message and showed some loving sympathy to the young man. Eventually, he happily cleaned up his act (literally) and the smell went away. Yet our love and respect for the young man's dignity remained.

Some young men in my mid-day classes frequently farted in class (often after eating lunch) and had a tendency to clear the seats nearby them. These instances were a bit different because we all get gas occasionally. Such disruptions were a bit funny and at the same time disgusting. I therefore encouraged those with gas to make a trip to the bathroom whenever they felt the need to relieve themselves.

Navigating through the many interpersonal situations as a teacher with your students requires tact and heart. You can't just do everything "by the book" and trample on hearts involved. Students want to be respected and esteemed by their peers. Therefore the way you speak to students must be sensitive and empowering.

If you fail to build up your students, you can quickly demoralize and devastate them. Once that happens, students can tend to hate you. These emotions lead to more resistance and defiance in the classroom. Therefore proactively uphold the honor, respect, and dignity of every student within your classroom. As you do, your students will simultaneously and mutually give you the respect you deserve (and need to successfully lead your classroom).

Paul in Manipur, India (a war zone within the country) where he spoke to this precious church and encouraged them.

As an educator often you are the only mother or father a child may know. Therefore as much as is within you try to be loving, gentle, and nurturing. These traits will work far better than merely trying to be the disciplinarian and get the job done.

We all inwardly starve for love and recognition. Life is not so easy sometimes. Therefore bring words of encouragement and comfort when necessary to sustain your students' spirits.

You never know what a child may be going through at home – sometimes worst than your wildest imagination. Therefore show compassion, be empathic, and understanding.

Of course this is easier said than done, but as you do the results will speak for themselves and your students will willingly endeavor to please you. The surest way to make a student an overachiever is to praise them when they do well. Praise and affirmation is contagious and something we desperately crave.

34. Motivate and Encourage Struggling Students

Struggling students come in all sorts. Students struggle academically for a variety of reasons. The means by which and methods to adequately address the academic needs of struggling students also vary.

What motivates students is different than what motivates teachers. It is humorous to watch teachers try to reason with students based upon motivating factors that students do not care about.

Teachers who are twenty and thirty years older than students often have great difficulty reasoning with them, as obviously these educators have forgotten what it is like to be that age.

Motivating youth therefore requires that educators be relatable to some degree and understand what is important to students. When I had a student struggling to do his assignments and classroom activities, I immediately recognized a bit of depression in his emotional makeup.

Seeking ways to enliven him (not just to learning, but to life in general), I decided to relocate him to sit next to some cheerful students who were always eager to do their assignments. The result proved to be transformational. Not only did this depressed young man come alive, but he also began turning in assignments and participating in class.

I guess the fact that I sat him next to some intelligent young ladies helped motivate him. These are the kind of modifications that sometimes are needed to bring about a paradigm shift and motivate your students.

Each student is uniquely different and requires special attention. I had to move other male students who couldn't do their work because of the ladies nearby who distracted them. Each situation and circumstance requires that a successful teacher be watchful and have a discerning heart to know what to do.

Paul at Karla's cousin's wedding in Toronto, Canada. Ontario is a lovely place to visit in the summer, but I think Paul would freeze to death if he were to be there in the winter.

One February when Paul was coming home from staying in Taiwan six months, he passed through Toronto for the night and said it was so cold he could feel the frigid winter air penetrate his bones.

35. Have a Level Playing Field for all Students

When you teach, be sure to keep a level playing field academically for all students. That means the star athlete has the same amount of requirements as the diligent bookworm. The principal's child gets no breaks because his mom is your boss. The cheerleader is not permitted to forego an assignment because she has to go compete in nationals.

The academic rigors must be the same for every student regardless of their personal struggles and extracurricular activities in which they participate.

Athletes are students first, without which they are not permitted to participate in school sports. The student that fails to keep his or her grades up cannot participate in sports. School therefore is to be the top priority. (This is not to say school is to be a student's life. Some educators act as if school is one's life and this is not correct either.)

Making exceptions should be done on a case-by-case basis as deemed appropriate. Yet such exceptions should not become common practice and abused. Otherwise students will bombard you with all of their excuses and reasons as to why they should be given exceptions.

Although it may hurt and pull on your heartstrings at times as a teacher, being fair to all students is most necessary to ensure academics are held in high regard above all other school related functions.

Paul with his three wonderful grandfathers.

Some kids aren't so lucky to even have a grandfather, but Paul got three! Ironically, two of them are also named Paul. Paul's maternal-grandfather standing behind him (a retired Lt. Colonel from the U.S. Army) of Slovakian descent Paul Krofchik; Paul's paternal-grandfather to his right (a building contractor) Merrill Davis; and Paul's stepmother's father Paul Andrea to his left (a writer and publisher) of Albanian descent.

Paul was raised by his maternal-grandfather standing behind him, as Paul's mother was an alcoholic and drug addict who couldn't seem to get her life together. Although having a mom who struggled with substance abuse was heartbreaking for Paul, he found great joy in his beloved grandparents who raised him. They were as Paul's very own beloved father and mother.

Even after Paul's father and stepmother got custody of him in the fifth grade, Paul often went home to be with his grandparents during the weekends as that is where his heart always remained. In fact Paul so loved his grandparents he actually cared for them in their old age rather than put them in a nursing home.

36. Establish Your Class Rules & Don't Deviate

From day one, you need to command and govern your classroom. Establishing your class rules to ensure a respectful teaching environment in which teacher and students' dignity is upheld is vital to your success as an educator.

Beware of trying to befriend and get your students to like you. As a teacher in the beginning work on establishing rules, boundaries, and achieving respectful conduct. Otherwise your students will run all over you and dominate the atmosphere, while dampening the learning focus. If you want academic success for your students, you have to rule your classroom with diligence and hold firmly to your guidelines.

Remember you get out and from students what you expect. Do not lower your expectations, because the minute you do students will respond accordingly. Commit to continuously apply positive pressure and make a demand upon your students to do their best academically. Consistently strive to maintain your learning focus and goals for your students.

Every teacher differs as to their class rules for students. I like to keep it simple myself. I basically had the following rules in my classroom:
- Respect your teacher and fellow students.
- Raise your hand when you want to speak.
- Honor and care for school property and books.
- No foul language or sexually inappropriate references.
- Be punctual and in your seat when the bell rings.
- Raise your hand when you want to speak.
- Do your assigned class work without making excuses, but ask for help when you need it.

Paul with the cast of the Broadway musical the Wedding Singer.

Get your Broadway tickets in a flash here below:

http://www.ezticketsearch.com/adtrack/?Event=Les+Miserables&AdTrack=EZAF0965224264

http://www.ezticketsearch.com/adtrack/?Event=Romeo+And+Juliet&AdTrack=EZAF0965224264

http://www.ezticketsearch.com/adtrack/?Event=Lion+King&AdTrack=EZAF0965224264

37. Welcome All Races, Ethnicities & Cultures

Whenever I received a new student throughout the year, I would always welcome them joyfully. Usually my new students were Hispanic, which means I would say, "Bienvenidos!"

It was always heartwarming to see the new students go from utter shock to instant relief, when they realized their Caucasian teacher could speak some Spanish.

I would immediately get to know their name (some pronunciations take longer than others) and try to become acquainted with them. If they were from a country I had traveled to, I would tell a story or mention some places within their nation where I had visited.

One way I best became acquainted with my students was by having them write an essay on their life dreams. This enabled me to know their hobbies, passions, and desired pursuits. Not to mention these essays were fun to read and allowed me to gauge students' level of mastery of the English language.

Many students surprised me with how well they could write in English and how profound their dreams were. I immediately gained a deep respect for all of my students. The result was incredible as I often addressed and referred to my students according to their future profession.

For example, if Susana wanted to be a doctor after high-school, I might call upon her in class once in a while by saying, "Doctor Susana, what do you think about this?" Susana in turn would smile real big because I recognized her and identified her future dream job, rather than just considering her merely as a student.

This kept the students actively engaged in class and consistently moving toward dream fulfillment. Welcoming students and continually being welcoming throughout the progress of your class during the year will warm students up to you and keep their hearts hot throughout the academic year.

It is worth noting going to school everyday for students is often no more thrilling than going to work everyday as a teacher. Therefore be kind as their teacher and avoid being condescending or seeming demanding. Reframe the rigors and academic demands via your assignments by reminding your students that this is another step in their professional and personal development you handpicked to prepare them for dream fulfillment.

By approaching classes and assignments as preparation for success in life, you will be amazed at the level of respect and intense focus students will give you during class. I often noticed when students became unruly that when I reminded them why we were doing a particular lesson was for their future development en route to dream fulfillment, suddenly a holy hush swept over the room as they regained their academic focus.

Paul eating mofongo in San Juan, Puerto Rico in the ritzy Candado district before a cruise to the western Caribbean.

Paul & Karla stayed at the Candado Plaza Hotel & Casino, where they had a lovely room overlooking the ocean.

For your next getaway, try one of these fabulous resorts: http://click.linksynergy.com/fs-bin/click?id=3RWH2TJD1YU&offerid=172314.10000030&type=3&subid=0

38. Speak A Few Words from Other Languages

By learning a few words commonly used in the languages and native tongues of your students, you will develop a deeper and more meaningful bond with them.

My first year teaching in an American public school was primarily with Latino and Haitian students, with the exception of one exchange student from China.

Tzo was a delightful young student from main land China, who was pleasantly surprised to hear that I had been to both China and Taiwan. In fact I attended Hong Kong University for an international law program one summer and lived in Taipei, Taiwan where I taught English for six months (until China threatened to bomb Taiwan – March, 1996 – when I came home).

My poor pronunciation of Mandarin (a difficult tonal language that has four inflections of the voice, all meaning something vastly different) was warmly received by Tzo, who had many laughs with me throughout the year when I had flashbacks of how to say a certain word in Chinese.

My Mandarin also impressed my Latin and Haitian students who also took an interest in learning how to say certain words. My pinyin provided me a simple way to pronounce Chinese words and expressions such as: "Wo ay ni!" (I love you!).

My trips to and tours through France were adequate enough to enable me to remember a few French words that made my Haitian students greatly rejoice.

Best of all however was my pronunciation of Spanish, as I studied this language for years throughout my schooling. I studied Spanish in high school, college, and University. Not to mention I have traveled from Mexico to Argentina. What was most challenging and difficult was speaking in churches without a translator in Ecuador, Cuba, and Venezuela.

Thankfully Latinos are very kind and forgiving people, who are eager to help you through your linguistic struggles to properly pronounce their language.

Therefore by showing my students I too am interested in their language and endeavoring to learn a few words (with their help) each week, we developed a deeper and more friendly connection. When seeking to learn a word or two from my students, I would call whoever taught me any given day my personal "maestro" (teacher).

Paul enjoying his bed at the Candado Plaza Hotel in PR.

Rest and relaxation is something teachers need to do more of. They often work too hard and get stressed out too much.

Put the joy back into your life by deciding to be happy everyday no matter what your students or administrators bring you.

Paul at the historic fort in San Juan, Puerto Rico overlooking the magnificent ocean and beautiful beach. Some of the best Caribbean cruises leave Puerto Rico.

39. Use & Integrate Modern Technology

Today's students are way ahead of the curve when it comes to knowing how to use the latest technology. As for me, I fall somewhere in the middle being up on some stuff, but lingering behind with other forms of technology.

My class research project for my first year of teaching consisted of a five page typed report in which students were allowed to choose between one of the following inventions to write about.
- Myspace
- Facebook
- Ipod
- Cell phone
- Airplane
- Automobile

This allowed students to choose a modern invention and describe how it has revolutionized the world. The research for ESOL students was remarkable as many mentioned aspects of each invention I had never before considered. Moreover each student learned the joys of researching and discovering interesting information about something they are passionate about.

Paul at about 10 years of age standing in front of his mother and alongside his baby brother, cousins, aunt & grandparents.

Being technologically savvy doesn't come easy for some of us who grew up in an age where there were only typewriters. I remember when I was in high school and took a computer class. I was absolutely clueless and just going through the motions. Truly I was faking it in route to making it. Thankfully I had some kind and patient friends who helped me along the way when it came to computers and science classes.

Today I can email, use various software programs, create and edit videos, format books, and many more things. Yet there is a lot I still cannot do and make an absolute mess of.

As a teacher you will greatly benefit from knowing how to use MS Excel spreadsheets and sort various lists according to the students within your classes. Incidentally, this is something I'm still not too good at.

My nonprofit organization does mailers throughout the year and sorting addresses for bulk rate mailing is a bit challenging for me, but I'm pressing on despite my initial knee jerk reaction and inclination to resist such technology.

Paul & Karla with the wonderful dining staff on Royal Caribbean Cruise Lines. If you'd like to know more about fabulous cruises go to cruise-options.com or write Paul.

40. Protect Your Privacy & Personal Property

Just because you are a schoolteacher and interact with your students very closely every day, does not mean they have the right to invade your personal space. One thing that disturbed and troubled me about my students was the casual nature by which they grabbed and removed supplies from my desk without first having asked permission to do so.

Unfortunately, many students come from broken homes and fractured families where parenting is not at the level it should be. That being said as a teacher sometimes you must teach your students proper manners and social graces, while simultaneously teaching your curriculum.

To neglect such is doing yourself and your students a grave disservice, because these life skills are necessary to ensure their success once they leave the four walls of school and enter the real world.

It is sad (if not sickening) to see how students speak and behave in school nowadays, but it is part of a teacher's job to model proper behavior and expect such from students. In all things, you get what you expect. Furthermore what you tolerate will continue to dominate.

Don't perpetuate your pain as a teacher when students seek to invade your privacy and carelessly without permission handle your personal property. Set proper perimeters early on and articulate your expectations clearly so kids know upfront what is permissible and intolerable.

Since the economic downturn has caused many families to lose their homes and parents to be laid off from their jobs, students have gotten sticky fingers in class and the cafeteria as they seek to cope and survive daily.

The world in which we live is becoming increasingly complicated and troubling for youth, but without strong leaders to guide and govern this generation they will self-destruct.

Never therefore feel bad when you have to play the role of the disciplinarian. Although it is not easy and seems a bit rough at times, in reality this is what is most needed in children's lives (especially those who have gone untrained and left without parental guidance to harness them).

Despite their bitter complaining initially and tendency to express their hatred of discipline (and sometimes you as a means of manipulation), know that kids deep down within ultimately desire proper boundaries and perimeters to provide a healthy atmosphere for them to grow. To deny your students this is to unnecessarily baby and pamper them, while allowing them to self-destruct.

Delayed gratification by reason of proper discipline is far better than immediate gratification that tends toward self-destruction.

Paul with the stars from the Broadway musical Legally Blonde.

http://www.ezticketsearch.com/adtrack/?Event=Legally+Blonde&AdTrack=EZAF0965224264

41. Cultivate Mutual Respect and Trust

I once blundered with my students when the pencil placed by the bathroom sign out sheet went missing. I didn't blatantly accuse my students of stealing it, but I did kind of let on that I perceived such.

By reason of past experience, many students came to class without paper and something to write with. Unbelievable I know, but this was a frequent occurrence among my ESOL students. Therefore often my students would pinch my pencil or pen to do their assignments (without permission the majority of the time).

Nevertheless I was incorrect in my assessment and accusation this time, as the next day when looking for something behind the bookshelf (whereon the sign out sheet and pencil had been placed) I found the missing pencil. My students immediately chirped up and let me have it, "See! We didn't take it."

I apologized and admitted the error of my ways, recognizing that I had foolishly jumped to conclusions instead of giving them the benefit of the doubt.

My father modeled humility during my childhood, by apologizing to me whenever he did something he later regretted or thought was inappropriate. Whether it was being temperamental, reacting hastily, or saying something unkind; dad was always humble hearted enough to make amends and apologize for his wrongdoing.

This gave me a tremendous respect for my father. Was he human? Absolutely! Yet his ability to be transparent and admit his flaws won my heart. Moreover my father has a great sense of humor and doesn't take himself too seriously.

I've tried to be the same with my students and yes, like my father sometimes I lose my temper with my students and angrily react. Nevertheless for the most part I'm somehow able to keep my students on task and don't have to resort to ruling over them with a heavy hand (most of the time :o).

Truly whatever we sow, we in turn shall reap. Therefore showing respect to your students is a good law to live by. The golden rule says to do unto others, as you would have them do unto you. This law of reciprocity truly will eventually boomerang back to you. It is prudent therefore to make sure as an educator you are projecting and sending forth the right signals to your students.

Paul & Karla aboard another fantastic cruise enjoying a night of outstanding entertainment aboard the ship.

http://www.ezticketsearch.com/tickets/results.cfm?Event=Cirque+du+Soleil:+Cirque+2009&AdTrack=EZAF0965224264

42. Allow Meaningful & Timely Discussions

When a student asks a meaningful question that is off task, even though it diverts attention from the curriculum and your lesson plan, take time to revisit and discuss it.

There are times throughout the year when breaking news, current events, and important societal issues are valuable for students to be discussed in class. Allow for such healthy disruptions to facilitate powerful teaching moments. Facilitate meaningful classroom discussions on the world issues of the day periodically, when your students need a fresh perspective and to be reminded why learning is important.

A passionate debate of ideas is always thought provoking. Let students take sides on issues and have a spirited intellectual debate, wherein they formulate and express their ideas.

The hot issues of contention in politics, religion, and world affairs are great topics of discussion and debate for students. Women's rights, abortion, euthanasia, gay rights, same sex marriage, freedom of religion, affirmative action, combating terrorism, foreign policy, constructive engagement diplomatically, environmental activism, animal rights, deforestation, global warming, political ideology, economic initiatives, recession, unemployment, gun rights, gender stereotypes, race discrimination, racial profiling by law enforcement, domestic abuse, child molesters, drug addiction, alcohol abuse, and corruption in government are just a few hot topics worthy of discussion.

http://www.ezticketsearch.com/adtrack/?Event=Bill+Cosby&AdTrack=EZAF0965224264

http://www.ezticketsearch.com/adtrack/?Event=Sean+Hannity+Freedom+Concert&AdTrack=EZAF0965224264

Paul in front of collapsed World Trade Center building #7 where he worked with the Salvation Army providing rescue relief the week of the terrorists attacked America.

Paul at Ground Zero in New York City the week of the attack.

43. Ask Questions & Listen to Students' Answers

Truly listening is a loving act and often the highest form of genuinely showing love in our fast paced world. Parents in this televised and technologically mesmerized world sometimes forget to disconnect from the many distractions that vie for their attention long enough to listen to and spend time with their children.

That being said, it should be no surprise students misbehave in class. Kids need to be heard and desperately yearn for someone of stature to listen to them. The youth of this generation have deep struggles and issues they are grappling with. They therefore need to process their pain and hear from the older generation what they should do.

What youth however will not do is take advice from somebody who does not care enough to first patiently listen to their hurts and pains. How can we expect youth to care about what we know, until they first know how much we care?

We as adults and educators rarely take advice from those we dislike. Unless a commonality, likeability, and level of heartfelt trust is first established; it is highly unlikely anybody will endeavor to hear from somebody no matter how wise they may be.

How often we miss it when we try to force feed youth with our rules, protocol, policies, and procedures. Often if we would just step back a bit and provide a heartfelt explanation as to why such rules are necessary and beneficial to us all, then students would be more apt to embrace rather than resist them.

Moreover if we as adults and educators actively engage and welcome the participation of our youth in the drafting of rules for our homes and classrooms, they will be more apt to emotionally buy into these established procedures since they participated in their formation.

Yet if we always treat kids as immature adolescents, they will assuredly live up to our expectations and choose a path of rebellion. Know this one thing for sure. Youth are very skilled at getting attention. The question is will our students be heard, actively engaged, and made participants so they can willingly cooperate with us or will we lord ourselves over them and alienate them? If we choose the latter, we can expect more rebellion and dissidence among our students.

Hence being an educator is a balancing act as we navigate between the interpersonal complexities and intricacies in leading and winning the hearts and minds of our students; and fulfilling our professional role in concert with the many demands of our county school board and administration.

Yet as we show students that we too can listen to them and ask meaningful questions to get their heartfelt answers, it will endear them to us and bridge the generation gap making our jobs far less difficult. Education in an era when violence and murder occurs in the classroom demands that we not only speak to our youths' minds, but also tenderly touch and respectfully connect with their hearts.

Karla & Paul in Fiji on their honeymoon enjoying a night of fun.

http://click.linksynergy.com/fs-bin/click?id=3RWH2TJD1YU&offerid=136622.10001068&type=3&subid=0

44. Respect & Encourage Differences of Opinion

One of the beauties of teaching ESOL is the variety of opinions a teacher can elicit from all of the many diverse nationalities present. Honestly, sometimes I feel like I have the best job in the world being able to hear from so many different ethnicities and students from different socio-economic backgrounds.

During President Obama's political campaign against Senator John McCain, our class discussions were very lively and passionate. I facilitated some wonderfully meaningful discussions (sometimes playing the devil's advocate) questioning my students why they favored a particular political candidate. Honestly, I deeply respected both men and felt either of the two would be good for our country.

By encouraging differences of opinion, I was able to learn a lot myself as the teacher. Getting beneath the skin and hearing from others is a valuable experience that teaches us all. I always tell my students they don't have to agree with each other, but they can always learn from and better understand one another.

This ability to speak maturely and engage each other respectfully in a passionate discussion is what being an adult is all about. Differences of opinion and ideological viewpoints will always exist throughout our lives (and often even within marriage). We as educators therefore owe it to our students to teach them how to disagree respectfully and simultaneously honor individuality and authenticity.

Diversity and variety makes life more enjoyable and fun. As it is true in regard to race, so too do diverse ideological views and opinions stretch us. Our minds are like rubber bands. They work best and perform at optimal levels when adequately stretched.

Cultivating self-respect and inner security, means we don't have to feel insecure when somebody of another opinion disagrees with us.

This is one thing I respect and greatly admire about President Obama. He masterfully and intelligently learns from his adversaries, while cultivating them relationally and drawing them near. Most alienate and aggravate their opponents, demonizing and distancing themselves from them. Our wise President however (at the time of this writing) respectfully entreats and humbly learns from his political opponents.

President Obama did a great job upholding Senator McCain and respecting the war veteran who bravely served our country. Following a grueling political campaign that led to the defeat of Senator McCain, a war hero, President Obama honored him and welcomed him to the White House to give his advice as to what direction he thought the country should take given the dire economic circumstances before us.

When President Obama made his first trip to Europe, unlike his predecessor, President Obama told world leaders: "I have not come to lecture, but to listen."

I think we can all benefit from following President Obama's fine example of humility and diplomacy whenever we find ourselves in the midst of differing opinions. Let us so teach our students to do likewise and behave in a dignified manner, rather than deride those they disagree with.

After all, we should never burn bridges, because life has a funny way of causing us all to later cross paths again. Truly none of us are as wise and strong as all of us. Therefore let our creed be less of "me" and more of "we".

45. Awaken the Dreamer & Visionary Within

One thing I always endeavor to inspire in all of my students is the dreamer within. I want to awaken the visionary in every human heart and take people on an internal dream voyage, where they explore the depths of their own heart and with childlike faith dare to live their dreams.

International students often intimately become acquainted with the quest of the American dream through their parents, who bravely venture beyond their shores and national borders to move to the United States. Yet upon arriving in our beloved country, they suddenly realize (along with their parents), that the American dream does not come on a silver platter.

On the contrary, the illustrious American dream is only realized daily and progressively as we put feet to our faith and bring our discipline to the level of our desires. Only when we behold our personal promised land within can we happily and consciously choose to persevere and push through our present struggles. Otherwise we would be overwhelmed and greatly discouraged when we walk by sight.

These brave souls who have left their beloved homeland and come from far and wide to make a new home for their families are incredible individuals. Often their children work alongside of them at night, following a rigorous day at school.

From sunrise to sunset they persevere determined to triumph and carve out for their families a new life. Such a work ethic and bold determination is a marvelous source of motivation for me personally.

As I quietly watch and attentively listen to these international students' stories, I am continually reminded of my many blessings (blessings many often take for granted).

Paul and Chris at Borobudur Temple in Java, Indonesia (one of the wonders of the world) standing with some ladies from Papua, who were giggling nonstop at the "bule" (white men) and were very desirous of having a picture taken with them.

Yet once the cameras were brought out, as is typical for Asians, all smiles were wiped off of their faces. Nevertheless the ladies were very pleased, personable, and welcoming.

The American stereotypes of Muslims abroad are often unwarranted and false. Fear always conjures up innumerable perceptions, most of which are erroneous and unsubstantiated. These ladies (and most Indonesians Paul has met over several trips to the world's largest Muslim populated nation) were very warm and welcoming.

If you'd like to help build bridges worldwide, support Paul by making a tax-exempt charitable contribution to:

Dream-Maker Ministries
PO Box 684, Goldenrod, FL 32733 USA
Paypal.com account – RevivingNations@yahoo.com

46. Encourage Organizational Skills for Success

Part of the reason students struggle immensely with their schoolwork is because they are disheveled and painfully disorganized. I often stop my students in class when I see them frantically searching for missing papers. I periodically remind my students the importance of being organized.

I simplify it by saying, "If you are organized enough to comb your hair and get beautified for school every morning, then you can organize yourself academically. If you can organize your cable television to record your favorite shows, then you can organize your life to do your homework. However if you fail to plan, you plan to fail."

It's funny to watch the light bulb within their brains come on as obviously nobody has ever spoken to them like this before. Yet if you continually baby high school students and treat them like children, you will perpetuate and prolong their incompetence and disorganization.

When students come to my class asking for paper and pens, I tell them, "I'm a teacher, not Walmart." If you have money to buy new shoes, fancy clothes, and gold chains then you can afford to go buy yourself some school supplies. Please do so as I will not be providing them daily for you."

It's a pleasure to see students make the paradigm shift and begin to act responsibly in regard to organizing their life. When they do, their grades and what I call "withitness" drastically improve.

Pampering students as a teacher can equate to crucifying and torturing yourself. Because what you tolerate will perpetuate and dominate. It is far better to be thought to be mean and demonized briefly by your students for not providing their every need, then to be aggravated daily with providing for them.

Karla holding an iguana in Curacao with Paul.

Karla was braver than Paul that day, as Paul was a bit iffy about the iguana and the local guy who owned it. Paul was having flashbacks of a story he heard on Fox News where actress Sharon Stone's husband was walking around barefoot in a California zoo, where Stone's hubby was bit by a deadly Komodo dragon.

Thankfully however this reptile in Curacao was harmless and made for a fun picture.

Try a fabulous cruise of your own sometime!

http://click.linksynergy.com/fs-bin/click?id=3RWH2TJD1YU&offerid=136622.10001096&type=3&subid=0

47. Promote Self Expression & Social Skills

Encourage students to speak freely during classroom discussions and uphold their opinions. By doing so you create a safe zone within your classroom and encourage intellectual discussions.

Moreover by facilitating meaningful discussions in class, you also teach students how to properly conduct themselves in social settings. Early on, I had to implement and enforce simple rules in my classroom like raising your hand before you speak. I also had to correct students for being rude and interrupting their classmates when they were talking.

Regulate your classroom by installing proper rules for verbal interaction and facilitating respectful guidelines for meaningful dialogue. By doing so, you create a respectful atmosphere in which students can listen and be heard by one another. This will cause them to be more attentive in class as their peers speak up and become intellectually engaged while giving their opinions on topics of interest.

For students who are a bit more inhibited and shy, gently nudge them daily and endeavor to pull them out of their shell. However beware of coming on too strong so as to terrify them, which will just make them more fearful. Be gentle and keep learning fun by being a bit playful when calling on more shy students.

Smile when calling upon your students, especially the more shy students so they feel loved and safe. By doing so, I have successfully been able to cultivate students desire to be more participatory in class.

Praise all answers and never blatantly say, "You're wrong." Instead say, "Good try, nearly." Or you can say, "Almost" (and smile) and ask for other students to answer.

Instead of lingering with the student whose answer was incorrect too long and making them feel uncomfortable, I immediately transition and call on the entire class saying, "Can anyone help or provide another answer?"

This keeps the question and answer classroom time lighthearted and more carefree, when students don't feel bad or belittled for being wrong. I like my students to believe failure is the key to success. Only by failing can we succeed. You only fail when don't dare to attempt.

We make advances by taking chances. We bear fruit by getting out on a limb. No guts, no glory.

Every great inventor was brutally ridiculed and laughed at before his or her invention came to full fruition. When you watch the old films of the Wright Brothers, you see their sheer determination and perseverance as they endured the creative process en route to perfecting the airplane.

Today because a couple men were willing to endure ridicule, mockery, and scorn we have amazing airplanes that take us all over the world.

Nowadays you can absolutely find a flight to anywhere in the world you want to go! Catch a last minute flight this weekend somewhere fun and save big!

http://click.linksynergy.com/fs-bin/click?id=3RWH2TJD1YU&offerid=136622.10001105&type=3&subid=0

By teaching your students to not take themselves too seriously, while simultaneously taking their education seriously, they will be more carefree and participatory in class. This makes for a fun, enriching, and empowering learning environment for all.

48. Encourage Composition & Creative Writing

By encouraging students to formulate their thoughts and compose them within written text, you allow them to best learn how to properly use language. As an English and ESOL teacher, I have found that through writing students often best learn the language.

Students who often are disinterested in texts written centuries before they were born find more enjoyment in being able to engage their own thoughts during the acquisition of language. By giving students the liberty to tell you about themselves and personalize the learning experience through freestyle writing assignments, you can get students to emotionally buy into your lessons and simultaneously as an educator you can best identify where they are in their acquisition and proper use of the language (or subject material).

I have found written essays to be far more revealing than the typical multiple-choice exam (a.k.a. "multiple guess" test as some students refer to them).

As an English teacher, I have been pleasantly surprised every time I gave my students liberty to write and fulfill academic requirements in essay form. Moreover my ESOL students took great joy in drafting and creating their own poetry.

My presumption initially was international students might be a bit resistant toward a poetry assignment. The opposite was true as they happily embraced the challenge to use the English language in a new manner. It became a very enjoyable lesson as students further became acquainted with the language and words that sound similar.

Playfully mixing up your daily routine and finding creative ways to engage students is always beneficial to the learning process. You can greatly enhance your classroom experience by eliciting information and feedback from your students through written essays. You will be amazed when you give your students opportunity to tell you what they know and how they see the learning experience.

Karla & Paul at Championsgate in Central Florida.
Paul is wearing a batik from Indonesia, a shirt Karla isn't overly thrilled about but Paul finds to be very comfortable in tropical climates and also somewhat stylish.

Yet both agree on their sunglasses for the Florida's sun:
http://click.linksynergy.com/fs-bin/click?id=3RWH2TJD1YU&offerid=161461.10000017&type=4&subid=0

49. Let Students Develop & Learn at Their Pace

No other subject and academic discipline demands as much sensitivity and individualized attention as ESOL. When teaching English as a second language to international students from afar, an extra level of sensitivity is necessary to get them to warm up to the language and not compare themselves with their peers who may be at a different level of language acquisition.

The same holds true in any academic subject. Students must be reminded that we all learn at a different pace. Unfortunately, the educational system as we know it, often just measures out grades based on performance. As a teacher however you can bridge the gap between different level learners by providing emotional support and encouraging every student no matter their level of mastery.

This will endear and encourage all students to do their best despite what their classmates may be accomplishing in class. Certainly we all take a shine to different subjects, topics, and interests. Otherwise we would merely be a conformist society. Therefore build on students' strengths rather than focusing on their weaknesses.

Praise and encourage students for their academic progress despite the pace and speed by which they make learning gains. As a teacher you always want to strive to make the learning progress positive and enjoyable. Otherwise you can unknowingly alienate your students and cause them to become disgruntled and to pull back from desiring to learn anything at all.

If failure looms large over them and overwhelms their soul, it is very likely they will emotionally pull back and checkout. This opens the door to innumerable disciplinary problems and class disruptions down the road.

Therefore do yourself and your students a favor by uplifting and encouraging each of them no matter the speed and pace by which they process and internalize the subject material. We all learn and respond at different levels of rapidity. Nevertheless the learning experience must remain positive and nurturing.

Paul & his brother-in-law Michael tearing into some turkey legs at Disney World's Magic Kingdom, after enduring several long lines and riding lots of kiddy rides.

When I was in Africa, I noticed how children eat with their parents. The meal is set in the middle of the family and everybody digs in. The children take smaller handfuls according to the size of their hands.

Likewise is it within education, teachers must allow students to mature and feed on enriching topical material at a pace in keeping with their academic ability. No matter how hard we as educators crack the whip and make demands, children can only process and retain so much information. Therefore give them some space and grace to do so. Plant the seeds for educational enrichment and let the students' minds cultivate them until they grow to full maturity.

Promote academic & athletic success with personalized magazine covers to praise students' accomplishments!
http://click.linksynergy.com/fs-bin/click?id=3RWH2TJD1YU&offerid=174146.10000044&subid=0&type=4

50. Be Honest & Admit When You're Wrong

Admitting when you have erred as an educator to respect and uphold your students will cause students to respect you. Kids realize teachers, like their parents, make mistakes. To deny and avoid recognizing this however smacks with pride.

Children and young adults dislike insincerity. On the other hand, kids draw near and dear to whoever can be real and admit their wrongs. Perhaps one of the reasons is because by being real and sincere about your flaws, it gives students hope for themselves. Nobody is perfect, but when we project an air of superiority we alienate people and make everyone feel uncomfortable.

Whenever my dad apologized for being harsh, cruel, and unkind to me I immediately forgave him. In fact, I respected him more for being a man and honestly acknowledging his wrongdoing. My father's humility caused me to love and trust him more. It showed me that if my dad became tough to deal with, he was thoughtful and reflective enough to perhaps later revisit his behavior and correct it.

When teachers project perfection however and rule with a heavy hand, it makes students immediately erect emotional walls of resistance. People relate more to reality rather than perfection. Being real and recognizing your failures won't encourage anarchy in your classroom. On the contrary, it will endear and actively engage your students to help improve the learning process. By listening to your students once in a while, you will be amazed at their ideas for implementing rules for classroom discipline, assignments, and homework.

Students genuinely want definable and easily understood structures that can daily guide them. Undoubtedly, following these rules and guidelines sometimes is difficult. Nevertheless having them in place maintains order and discipline, while being good for both teachers and students alike.

Paul in Singapore with some friends at City Harvest Church.

Singapore is a wonderful country full of many ethnicities and a rich diversity, not to mention it is very cosmopolitan and a hub for international business and global trade.

Love rejoices in the truth. We can do nothing against the truth but for the truth. Therefore let us as teachers fall on our own swords when necessary to let truth prevail. We shall all falter and fail at times, but if we uphold truth and honestly admit the error of our ways, we shall be able to maintain integrity of heart and show our students a better way.

The law of love upholds truth even when it is you who gets egg on your face and has to bite the bullet. I am the least qualified person to be writing this book, but because I genuinely want to help future educators succeed I die to my ego and continue to write.

Truth is liberating as is admitting to students once in a while that you messed up. Kids aren't perfect and they certainly understand it when you're not.

51. Be Compassionate to Students

The many rules at the high school where I taught were quite demanding for the students. For example, students had about 10 minutes between classes to go to the bathroom, go to their lockers, and walk to their next class.

The campus was rather large and spread out with several buildings. Students coming from the gym or auditorium had a substantial distance to walk. Not to mention teachers were instructed to teach from bell to bell.

This did not leave students much time to put away their books and folders, pack up their bags when the bell rang, and get to class. Amazingly however most students managed to get to class on time, although quite a few were literally running to do so.

The difficulty was once in class, students were continually asking to go to the bathroom. Therefore classes were being disrupted for bathroom breaks and other personal matters.

As a teacher I myself found it difficult to get to the bathroom and return to class on time. Considering I was the last one to leave the room after all of my students (and some students lingered to talk to each other), clearing my room and locking the door (to protect school property and my personal valuables) took some time.

Once I finally got to the teachers' break room, wherein was one bathroom, many times somebody else was using it. I therefore was made to wait a bit more. Hence my bathroom break was quickly gone and it was no longer a break, but what I considered a torturous experience.

Trying to hurry and go to the bathroom is not a delightful experience. Not to mention sometimes I barely had time to flush the toilet and wash my hands before the bell was about to ring.

When considering between washing my hands or getting to class on time to preserve my job, I often chose the latter. Thankfully the majority of the time I endeavored to go to the bathroom nobody was in there. Yet a good number of times the bathroom was occupied. Hence I had compassion on my students as they too only had one bathroom in my building to use and their peers often were in it when they needed it the most.

Sometimes jokingly I would say to my students who interrupted my class to ask permission to go to the bathroom, "Yes, you may go to the bathroom. Please go for me also."

Showing a bit of compassion and having a sense of humor makes long days bearable and students more pleasant to deal with over the long term. If however you choose to be a heartless legalist and do everything by the book, your students may come to resent you and become all the more rebellious.

Therefore give thoughtful consideration to your disciplinary plan, enforcement measures, and what exceptions you will permit and make allowances for.

As a male teacher, I can only imagine the potential lawsuits and parent complaints that could have arisen had I refused female students in high school permission to go to the bathroom. Therefore keep everything in perspective before you become callous and overbearing when ruling your students.

Sometimes it is better to lose a battle or two in order to win the war. Cultivating and nurturing good relations with your students is as important as providing a good education, because neither are mutually exclusive as they both work together hand in hand.

My experience has been whenever I angered and alienated a student over a trivial matter, it usually took some time afterward to get them back on track academically.

Therefore be mindful of the big picture rather than fixating on the minute details of discipline and school policies. I guess what I am trying to say is uphold the spirit of the law (or rules and regulations), but beware of being a heartless legalist who never makes exceptions to help human beings.

We as educators must remember students are also human beings. How would you feel if somebody denied you your basic human right to go to the bathroom? Therefore try to keep things in perspective and verbalize alternatives for your students so they can get their business done before your class, while knowing your expectations beforehand.

When one of my male students disappeared for 13 minutes on a bathroom break, I popped my head outside of my class and found him on a computer in the media center. I had not given him permission to use the computer. I therefore immediately filed a discipline referral that day noting his disrespectful behavior.

Tough love is also compassionate and never should you think otherwise. It is tough love and adhering to school policies that ensures student success academically. School policies and procedures have been put in place for a reason. They are often proven by reason of years of being tested and tried. Therefore don't try to reinvent the wheel. Just adhere willingly with the best of your ability and endeavor to get your students to comply also.

Never belittle school rules and policies. If you do, you send a message to your students that anarchy and rebellion is permissible. This will open the floodgates to more unruly and undisciplined behavior. Therefore do yourself a favor and outwardly honor and enforce school rules, despite what you inwardly may think of them.

Then when you chose to make that rare exception, you are not welcoming widespread rebellion by your students. Keep order in all things and govern your classes with strength consistently. Otherwise students will walk all over you and take advantage of your generosity.

Remember kids are master manipulators and skilled at getting what they want. After all children and students being provided for by their parents usually have no source of income, which means most of what they get they obtain by asking or charming somewhat who possesses what they want (or the ability to buy it for them).

One thing North American youth lack however is an understanding and value of hard work, along with the great personal sacrifice that goes into all of those little goodies they so badly want. Until somebody says no to a child or student it is unlikely they will value what they are accustomed to getting without any personal sacrifice.

Sometimes being compassionate means withholding from students to teach them to value personal sacrifice.

Karla & Paul at Rif Fort in Curacao during a Caribbean cruise.

52. Promote Identity Beyond Appearances

Youth all across America (and much of the world) are being bombarded by way of the media (predominately through TV) to dress a certain way to obtain the approval of their peers and achieve a desired popularity.

We as educators however must remind and teach our students that what someone is inwardly is what truly solidifies and establishes their identity. What one is inwardly is far more valuable than how they dress and clothe themselves outwardly.

This discovery however does not come easily to young people who are ridiculed and laughed at by their peers for what they wear. I recall a season in my youth when I lived with my father and stepmother in a doublewide trailer far out in the country. We had very little money and my clothes were a bit shabby.

In comparison with my friends' clothing, I felt a bit awkward and inferior socially. Nevertheless I tried to not let my look, as in what I was wearing, hinder my inner life.

The same holds true for outward beauty and being handsome. Some of us are not as gifted as others physically. We therefore can make up for our average (or below average) physical appearance by excelling in other areas of our life. For example, we can have a keen and lively mind to provide stimulating intellectual conversation.

As for myself, I excelled in playing baseball – which I did day and night from my boyhood until I finished high school. My identity soon revolved around my ability to play on the baseball diamond.

Although such an identity is a bit fragile and unstable, for me it was all I at the time knew. My identity as an athlete sustained me when I felt miserable within around my stepmother and inferior to my classmates because of my outward appearance (and family's economic status).

Thankfully there are always teachers who overhear students competing and bickering over clothes, who intervene when they hear kids foolishly fixating on and comparing who has the best threads amongst themselves.

53. Avoid Being Judgmental and Presumptuous

Sadly, it is so easy to be judgmental. It seems like being judgmental and accusatory comes rather easy for human beings. We unfortunately can tend to think the worst about others before fully knowing the facts.

This can lead to friction relationally (personally and professionally) and further intensify the problems we already have in our lives. Try therefore to give people the benefit of the doubt until you know all of the facts.

Avoid speaking prematurely and hastily, lest you have to later come back and apologize for being arrogantly and erroneously judgmental. Show some mercy and grace to others, realizing you too will need the same kindness sometime in your future.

American & Canadian celebrating July 4th at Rock Springs.

54. Don't Put Your Map on Students & Staff

As an educator always be careful not to put your map on your students. That means resist the urge and tendency to map out students' careers for them. Resist the tendency to send gentle hints and subtleties at career choices you would like them to pursue.

Parents rarely succeed when they try to put their map on their kids and make them play a particular sport. Immediately parental expectations take the fun out of the game. You too as a teacher, if you are not careful, can overly pressure your students and take the fun out of learning.

Therefore be careful and wholeheartedly attentive to every individual student's personal needs. Get to know your students' desires, dreams, and aspirations.

When you speak to your students, ask more powerful and thought provoking questions. As you do, you shall empower your students to be more self-aware and purposeful in their lives.

Let your students curiously and spontaneously come to a place of self-discovery. It will happen gradually and progressively throughout the totality of their lives. Never try to rush it. Of course often you will see things and want to communicate certain truths.

Nevertheless unless the light bulb within them turns on, you are speaking to deaf ears and dull hearts. Therefore pray for inward illumination so your students can perceive and apprehend what you are talking about.

Otherwise you will find yourself hitting up against a brick wall and make little progress with them. Always remember life is a discovery process and as you make discoveries, discerning new things about your students, they too will simultaneously make new discoveries about themselves as you spontaneously yield to the inner inspiration to take a few tangents to communicate vital truths to them.

Maturity comes about progressively. Maturation is a process, which cannot be rushed by us no matter how eager as educators we may be. Remember how immature you were, when you were a student in school. This is helpful to do occasionally to keep things in perspective and remember the audience to whom you are communicating.

Like a seed that goes into the ground and is left to the soil and elements to grow, so also must an educator's words often be. As difficult as this may seem, any farmer can tell you there is a healthy emotional detachment you must have to maintain your sanity after your work has been done and your words spoken.

Maturity requires initiative, endurance, and capacity. As an educator your personal maturation process will unfold as you develop the ability to take initiative in the lives of your students, the stamina to endure the difficult times when you feel like you want to quit (something I've felt hundreds of times), and the strength to attend to the numerous things being put upon you (personally and professionally).

As you feel yourself being stretched, know you are simultaneously growing. It may not always feel good. Sometimes you may feel as if you are in a funk and get that look of comatose that educators often have on their faces.

Cultivate your inner strength and don't allow the responsibilities of your job to get to you. Walk by faith and not by feeling or sight when you feel overwhelmed. Persevere through the mental and physical sluggishness. Go home after work and take a nap whenever you need to.

Likewise encourage your students on Friday afternoon to go home, forget about the books for a while, and enjoy their lives. We all must learn to live balanced lives so that we may be more blessed in all we do.

We live to enjoy life. Although education is our occupation as teachers, we must be mindful that education itself is not life. Sometimes you would not think this to be so based on the emotional investment and enthusiasm some educators put into their work – occasionally to the extent of appearing like they may not have a life apart from their job.

Don't get me wrong. Teachers who are most passionate and emotionally invested in their occupation tend to captivate and educate students the best. Yet outside of the classroom, if these educators do not live fulfilling lives, eventually it will show on their countenance and be transmitted to their students.

Our lives must be more full and well rounded if we are to be able to sustain life in the classroom over the long term. Otherwise eventually we ourselves will break down and become bitter.

The best teachers master the art of balancing a healthy profession along with a fulfilling personal life. In so doing, they successfully exemplify this principle to their students, who in turn follow in their footsteps. In simplicity, you cannot give what you do not have or possess.

Therefore as educators it is needful that we wholeheartedly give ourselves to the task of educating our youth, but at the end of the day also give ourselves freedom to live happy lives of our own.

By not allowing administrators and the county school board to fully monopolize and absorb your life, you in turn will be free and able to flourish in the classroom as an educator. Not so if you can't say no and allow everybody to overextend you and spread you thin. Beware of being used and abused by reason of not being able to say no and over committing to that which is beyond your ability.

Abide in your calling and remain focused on that which you enjoy and do well. As you do, you will not just survive, but happily thrive and stay inwardly alive.

Paul consoling a young man at a youth conference in San Jose.

We never know what the students we teach are going through in their personal lives, neither what they have been through up until now.

Many of us are hardened by life's circumstances that come upon us without invitation. Yet deep down within, there is a tenderness of heart waiting to be awakened and revived.

Upon watching Glen Close do a special report on Oprah about *Puppies for Prisoners*, it was remarkable to see inmates feel love for the first time in years. The quiet, unassuming, and unconditional love of a puppy melted these hardened inmates within and transformed their demeanor.

As the inmates were given the responsibility to train their assigned puppy, they felt a sense of responsibility they had not felt in years while being locked up. Truly if given the opportunity, anybody can again feel love and view life differently, whereby they can be transformed entirely.

55. Be Patient & Understanding

Give people the benefit of the doubt before you presumptuously assume and make judgments about things you know nothing about. You never know what a student, fellow teacher, dean, or administrator may be going through personally.

Before making a harsh statement you will later regret and have to apologize for, show some patience and understanding. Judge nothing before the time. Let things slowly show themselves and be brought to the light.

Beware of trying to be the hammer in the toolbox. You've been hired to be a teacher. Do that and do it well, rather than getting engaged in things beyond your job description. Maintain your focus and fight to keep a tender heart. Don't let your spirit be polluted by gossip during lunch, bathroom breaks, and staff meetings.

Be patient with your students remembering the many demands they are juggling. Studying for several classes, while participating in extracurricular activities (and still trying to have a bit of a social life to enjoy your friends) is no easy task. Not to mention hormonal changes and challenges can be difficult for students to manage. Raging hormones aren't easy to deal with when trying to study in class or do your homework at night.

In regard to patience and understanding, occasionally a student may approach you with a personal problem. Try to drop what you are doing, or ask the student to visit you after class (or at an appropriate time) to discuss the matter. When you do, take time to actively and attentively listen. More than speaking and trying to solve a student's problem, by just listening you will accomplish far more than you ever could think to do by giving advice.

Youth desperately long for a sympathetic ear and an attentive heart to unconditionally love and listen to them. As you do, you shall endear your students to you and cause them to freely open up to you.

This will pave the way for your words to carry weight when you speak. Truly, listening is loving at its finest. Sadly many in this present and younger generation don't get a sympathetic ear from their parents. They must compete with the TV, siblings, dinner, chores being done, cell phones, answer machines, visiting relatives, church demands, home ownership associations, and much more.

You as a teacher might be the only person who ever genuinely and attentively listens to a child. When this opportunity comes, eliminate all distractions, and respond attentively. Simply listen, love unconditionally, and refrain from putting your map on your students by way of giving unsolicited advice. Instead sometimes wait for your students to cultivate intellectual curiosity and ask you meaningful questions leading into those deeper conversations.

Paul with his friends Gaston & Juan Pablo in Argentina.

56. Look, Listen and Feel

As a lifeguard I was taught by the YMCA in a rescue situation to "look, listen, and feel" prior to conducting CPR. This simple three-step approach also works well for educators.

Teachers need to be attentive and responsive to students needs. When you welcome your students upon their arrival to class, look at their faces.

Some will be happy and eager. Other students will look disgusted and depressed. A few students will appear tired and haggard. Perhaps a few students will be excessively loud and unruly.

Immediately you must respond to all of these different emotional energy levels before you to properly direct your students. Great educators don't just teach, they also connect and inspire their students. They are somewhat of a cheerleader and coach, able to give a quick pep talk and reign in all of the students to focus on the task at hand.

Beyond looking, you will need to listen. Hear the objectives and complaints of your students. Listen to their challenges and difficulties with your educational style and assignments. Then listen even more attentively to lingering problems beyond the classroom adversely affecting your students emotionally and thereby educationally indirectly.

As you thereafter feel, you will be able to best relate and heal all of these wounds resident within your classroom. If nothing more than a kind or considerate word, speak in such a way to your students whenever you can. Your compassion and ability to feel will work wonders and heal.

Students like a teacher who has the ability to not just think, but also genuinely feel for them. Feelings go deeper and always surpass the mental arena and faculties.

Paul & Isai with a Muslim young man in Banda Aceh, Indonesia who lost his house as a result of the devastating tsunamis that swept through and leveled everything in sight killing over 200,000 people in just the island of Sumatra.

Paul & Isai were able to help finance the beginning stages of the rebuilding of this man's home and provided him a good size tent to put his family in while they awaited the completion of the construction. Hearing stories of survivors such as this young man was an inspiration, not to mention his determination to fearlessly rebuild was exemplary.

Upon hearing and seeing the tragic catastrophe on television in Paris, France on December 26th Paul immediately felt in his heart that he wanted to return to Indonesia (one of his favorite countries on earth) and help in the disaster relief effort. A few months later when Paul arrived in Banda Aceh, his translators informed him that the dead were still being buried.

One boy was throwing starfish back into the water, when an elderly man said to him, "You can't save them all boy!" The young lad replied, "Maybe not, but I can help save this one."

Make your life count for someone!

57. Breathe Deeply Often to De-Stress & Rest

Take a deep breath whenever you feel yourself getting stressed out and overwhelmed. Often just when I felt like I had gotten a handle on everything within the classroom (disciplining and controlling kids, grading papers, giving assignments, explaining expectations, and repeating my requirements to the students who don't usually listen the first time), then I would receive and email from administration asking me to do something more.

Inside I often felt one of three things: 1. I wanted to scream, 2. I wanted to quit, or 3. I wanted to tell administration where to go.

Neither of these three options served me, my students, or administrators well. I therefore remained quiet, but felt like I was being stretched beyond measure and dying inside.

I suppose what I was dying to was the need to always be in control and foresee everything coming my way. As a teacher, you need to be flexible and adaptable at any given moment to comply with administrators' requests and requirements.

When you don't have much time, but desperately feel within like you need a break from all of the demands and aggravation of teaching: simply take a deep breath and exhale slowly. Neurologically it truly does help relieve tension and regain your center of control. Moreover it helps you calm down and be whole realizing that it is just a job and it need not all be done in a day.

Chunk it down into bite size pieces and keep your composure. Resist the urge to complain verbally or in writing to other teachers or peers. Conserve your energy and simply accept what is before you. As you do, you will become increasingly resourceful and creative to conquer every challenge demanded of you.

Breathe deeply whenever and as often as you can. Breathe deeply whenever you take a quick trip to the bathroom, go to lunch, await the arrival of your students, dismiss class, prepare to speak to an administrator or parent, and walk from and to your car.

This simple exercise will help you to be fully present, while simultaneously empowering you. Breathing deeply helps you regain your center, reconnect with the Source of life, and calm your nerves that often are being aggravated by external stimuli beyond your control. Breathe deeply to reconnect, be empowered, and be made whole.

Paul with Chris & Angela after officiating their wedding. Chris with James Bond style blazed by boat on to the shore of his lakefront estate, barefoot, and ready to sweep Angela off her feet when the two were married.
www.itietheknot.com

58. Accept What and Those You Cannot Change

As a teacher within a school, county school board, and educational system at large you must keep things within perspective lest you be overwhelmed and exhaust yourself.

Remember your job description is that of a teacher. Therefore you need not worry about trivialities or big problems at a larger scale beyond your jurisdiction and assigned duty.

Certainly once you become a veteran teacher and learn the ins and outs of the educational system, should you want to become proactive and be an agent for change – by all means go for it!

Yet the first year is usually tough enough just trying to adjust and adapt to your new professional assignment and the rigors therein.

I myself often saw things that I didn't agree with, or thought could have been done differently or better. Nevertheless I continually reminded myself that which I had been hired to do. To trouble myself otherwise and allow myself to become entangled in numerous other battles and struggles would have distracted me from teaching.

I therefore chose to do one thing well, rather than spread myself thin and seek to tackle innumerable challenges beyond my capacity, and to perform it with excellence.

Since I did not earn an education degree, I transitioned from professional motivational speaking into teaching. Therefore the transition was a bit more demanding and challenging for me personally. Perhaps for you teaching is a piece of cake. If so, then feel free to give administration, legislation, and school board initiatives a go!

As for me however I immediately knew my limitations and chose not to overextend myself. I was already exhausted enough at the end of the day. Any more weight in my backpack would have done me in. Therefore instead of walking off of the cliff, I chose to walk steadily and slowly abiding in my calling as that of a teacher (at least for the academic year I committed to).

Paul with some charming Indian boys in a village deep in curry country. India is a nation Paul has lived in and traveled throughout, even returning five times to speak and minister in this great land.

The Ayurveda essential oils, massage techniques, and aromatherapy in India is sensational for personal rejuvenation. Even if you don't care for spas, bliss your body at home!
http://click.linksynergy.com/fs-bin/click?id=3RWH2TJD1YU&offerid=141101.10000096&type=4&subid=0

The air in the remote villages and tea plantations was so pure, you could breathe deeply without the obstruction of pollutants or harmful contaminants.

I guess in the city and suburbs we have to settle for air purifiers to reduce nasal congestion, open airways, and stop snoring.
http://click.linksynergy.com/fs-bin/click?id=3RWH2TJD1YU&offerid=170507.10000022&type=3&subid=0

59. Die to Your Ego & the Control Freak in You

If you've got a bit of a control freak in you and feel everything has to be done your way, as a teacher your pride will quickly be confronted by administration. When you overstep your boundaries and get put in your place, you can react one of two ways.

You can humbly swallow your pride and do as you're told (my choice), or you can arrogantly defend yourself. I try to avoid the latter because it just creates more friction and further intensifies internal hostility against you as an educator.

I have enough difficulties to deal with in the classroom. I don't need any more enemies outside the classroom. Trying to exert your influence prematurely before serving and winning the trust of your administrators first can bring about a detrimental blow to your ego when the powers that be confront you. Tread softly early on as an educator.

I would rather fall on the rock early on and be broken, than have the rock of authority fall on me later and crush me. Some administrators' managerial philosophy is such that they confront teachers openly and not privately. Therefore know the personality types presiding over you and how they respond to internal organizational conflict.

Perhaps my *Conflict Resolution* book can be of help. Many corporations and organizations bring me in to conduct an entire seminar on this sort of thing to minimize workplace conflict, improve employee morale, and enhance productivity.

If your school board budget can't afford a seminar on conflict resolution to increase productivity, try super food for your employees!

http://click.linksynergy.com/fs-bin/click?id=3RWH2TJD1YU&offerid=176136.10000004&type=4&subid=0

http://click.linksynergy.com/fs-bin/click?id=3RWH2TJD1YU&offerid=164905.10000095&type=3&subid=0

Paul with some smart and bright-eyed schoolboys in India at an academic institution, where Paul spoke an inspiring message to encourage their hearts. The schoolmasters in Chennai and Mumbai were very welcoming and eager to have Paul speak to their youth. The youth responded wonderfully and showed an impressive amount of manners during the presentation.

60. Speak Softly When Appropriate to Disarm

Before reacting emotionally in any given situation and raising your voice, try to be sensitive and respond softly. Often by doing so, you can show the other individual (perhaps a student, fellow teacher, or administrator) that you are a caring soul and gently win them to your side peaceably.

Gentle disarmament is a far better approach than hostility and aggressively escalating a conflict. Instead of pouring fuel on the fire, simply pull back and refocus your energies elsewhere.

Whenever fellow teachers want to engage in gossip, I remove and withdraw myself. Make up an excuse that you have to get back to class, go to the bathroom, or phone a parent. Refuse to engage in meaningless and destructive gossip. Gossip never changes anything and it always wastes your time.

Disarm your students by using some humor and reacting otherwise than they would have expected given the circumstances. As you intuitively recognize the best way to respond in any given situation, acknowledge the dynamic of your class and makeup of the personalities present you will discern the appropriate way to handle any given situation.

Paul with his dad and mother enjoying a laugh. Laughter, intellectualism, and sarcasm all run deep in Paul's family. Yet there is also much heartfelt love and sincerity.

Paul & Karla in lovely Fiji enjoying their honeymoon.

Undoubtedly a soft and sweet voice can disarm anybody. Certainly Karla's soft voice and gentle approach can melt me within.

While I was ministering throughout several churches in France, a few men were caring enough to try to speak into my life and provide some insight. In my arrogance, I didn't fully hear them. When however an elderly woman approached me as a mother and whispered in a gentle voice, I listened intently and took to heart every word.

Her gentle approach endeared my heart and melted my defenses. A tenderness of spirit like this cannot be faked, but must be felt. If however we were to lay down our agenda or quiet our egos, we too could find better ways of dealing with our problematic students. Truly wisdom is better than strength. After all it is the forceful approach (often resisted) that most wears us out and leaves us feeling exhausted as educators. Therefore try a more gentle approach to see results.

61. Express Your Emotions Gently Nonverbally

Better than speaking sometimes to address a student's misbehavior is to simply walk over to his or her desk and allow your proximity to speak for itself. By drawing closer to a problematic student, often this is sufficient to quiet and calm them down.

Other nonverbal cues can be touching the pencil a student is playing the drums with. Many annoyances can be silenced by gently approaching the troublemaker disrupting the entire class.

Asking a student who is talking to relocate to another side of the room apart from their friend is another wonderful way to quietly deal with a problem.

Paul with an adorable Pakistani boy named Bunti, who took a shine to Paul during his time speaking in Faisalabad.

Paul and friends in Moscow, Russia at Red Square.

The former Soviet Union is an intriguing place full of life. Just free from communism's controlling grip in 1992 and awakened by the Spirit, following our visit to Moscow University, the students triumphantly celebrated and chased our bus with joy!

Meeting so many friendly people throughout the world is an incredible experience and makes you want to phone once and a while to stay in touch. Yet when times are hard, every dollar counts. For great international calls at reasonable rates, Paul recommends:

http://click.linksynergy.com/fs-bin/click?id=3RWH2TJD1YU&offerid=121997.10000227&type=3&subid=0

62. Remind Students of Their Dreams & Need for Discipline to Experience Dream Fulfillment

Periodically throughout the year you will need to revisit and remind students of their dreams. As you do, regain students' focus on the importance of cultivating daily discipline so as to realize and fulfill their dreams.

We all have dreams, but the majority of us fail to fulfill and realize our dreams because of lack of discipline. Emphasize and stress the importance for daily discipline, focus, endurance, and determination to hold to the blueprint mapped out en route to dream fulfillment.

Laziness can easily overtake and overcome the best of us. Therefore we need accountability to keep us on task and moving forward. Encourage your students to choose and find an accountability partner to help keep them on track en route to fulfilling their dreams.

Paul doing some shopping in Dubai, UAE made some friends.

Paul on the grounds at the Borobudur Temple in Java, Indonesia after taking off his rice field worker hat.

One thing is for sure with so many women educators and administrators serving at schools, the quickest way to make friends and influence people is to show up with some delicious chocolates. For some of the best chocolate in the world, including raw organic chocolate to pick the ladies up:

http://click.linksynergy.com/fs-bin/click?id=3RWH2TJD1YU&offerid=171713.10000025&type=3&subid=0

63. Encourage Student Self-Investment

Encourage your students to be proactive about investing in themselves. Teach your students that the surest way to improve their standing in life is by the books they read and the people they associate with.

Undoubtedly, our friends will determine our future. Therefore we must beware of our associations and how we align ourselves socially.

Although we may never meet certain famous people, we can read their books and get into their minds. Books are fabulous tools to help us learn about famous people's secrets of success and how they achieved greatness.

Teach your students to be proactive and take initiative to learn what is most important to them, rather than wait upon serendipity and divine intervention to bring about their destiny. Instead of waiting for your ship to come in, swim out to sea to meet it!

Small girls in Pakistan forced into manual labor make bricks.

Encourage your students to travel the world, one of the best and most enjoyable investments they can make in themselves while having a wonderful experience.

Here is a travel special for students:
http://click.linksynergy.com/fs-bin/click?id=3RWH2TJD1YU&offerid=128469.10000022&type=4&subid=0

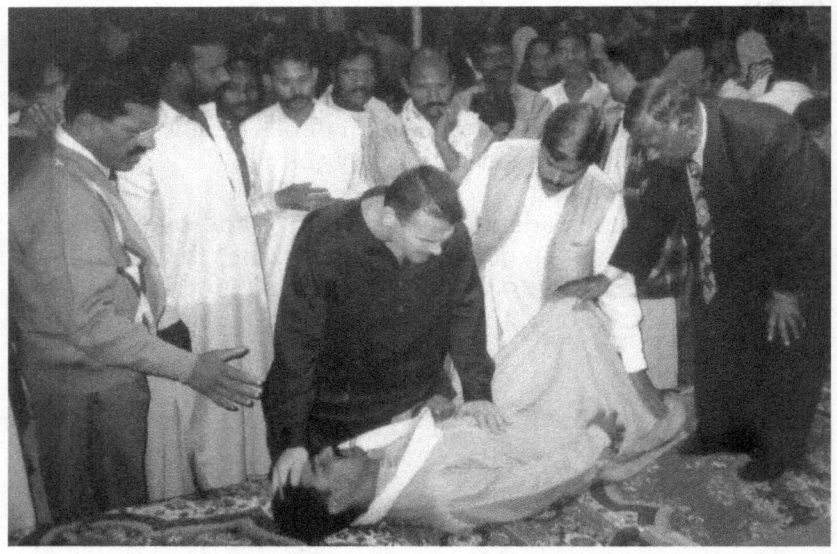

Paul praying for a man in Pakistan who was physically suffering. To Paul's amazement, after receiving prayer the man leapt to his feet and began to celebrate saying he suddenly felt better. To God be the glory for intervening to help hurting humanity and responding to our childlike faith.

A scene like this reminds me that we are all people with similar needs and struggles. No matter how much the American media or military-industrial-complex may demonize terrorists abroad, even U.S. military generals and commanders say the solution for war-torn nations is not more war and military invasions or occupations. A non-military solution is needed to achieve lasting peace in war-torn regions.

64. Don't Defend Yourself

I learned over time that people usually don't want to hear your side of the story. If they sincerely do, they will ask you. Therefore save yourself the time and aggravation. Don't get embroiled in fruitless discussions to defend yourself, when people don't care to hear your side of the story.

When I served as a proctor for the FCAT exam, there were some flaws in the script given to teachers presiding over the examination in their respective rooms. Although a day or two before I sought to question my principal and mentor about this, I received no answer, nor specific instruction to resolve my confusion. I was told to "read the email" and follow the script.

Like my students to some extent, I didn't fully understand that which was written. So I asked for help. When I received none, I had no other choice but to proceed haphazardly and blindly believe everything would be all right. Unfortunately, in this instance everything did not work itself out (at least not to the benefit of my students and myself).

I blundered and fumbled, making a bit of a mess of the test taking experience for my students. Following the printed script (as instructed by my principal), I stopped the test taking at 11:20am and waited for further instructions.

Upon doing so, the classroom of Haitian and Latino students began to get a bit unruly and loud. This is to be expected when students have nothing to do. Nevertheless I felt uneasy about the written directive and attempted to question a nearby dean in the building hallway, who had been monitoring students going to the bathrooms to ensure there was no cheating or test taking irregularities.

She told me it was her understanding that the ESOL students were to continue unabated and not stop, as their exams were not timed as the rest of the school. Yet I was so afraid of getting the hammer if I deviated from the written script, that I decided to follow it to the tee and "wait for further instructions" over the intercom.

When my principal passed by and entered the classroom I had been assigned for test taking, naturally she was livid. I too was a bit puzzled and disgruntled at the whole test taking procedures I had been given on a green script. Nevertheless in the past whenever I questioned anything, I was always firmly told to "read the email" and follow the written guidelines.

Doing so during the FCAT didn't serve me very well. At the end of the day, when I was called to the principal's office, I knew it was going to be nasty and I would be reprimanded sternly. To my surprise my principal had highlighted a portion of the script she was intent on focusing upon in our meeting (a meeting in which I was also surrounded by other deans and the FCAT head facilitator who was my teaching mentor). I had only wished she had taken a few seconds the day before (when I asked for help) to highlight her focal point on the lengthy script.

The meeting was short and to the point. My principal said, "Mr. Davis, what does the highlighted text say?" I basically read it as asked to do. After answering another question or two (similarly structured to ensure the desirable answer), the principal dismissed the jury. I then was left with she and the assistant principal (a more understanding and amicable fellow, who nevertheless was annoyed by my failure that day as a proctor ...which may have kept some students from graduating had they not finished the exam, which thankfully they did).

The hammering continued and I simply kept my mouth shut, as I was never asked to speak, nor given the liberty to provide my side of the story. My characterization of the events and previous attempt to seek clarification before the day of the exam was not permitted as a topic of discussion. Neither was I given opportunity to speak along those lines.

Knowing I had already screwed up, I just tried to be compliant and keep my mouth shut. Yet I knew there was some contributory negligence involved and my mother (a retired school teacher) assured me as a new teacher I shouldn't have been made to preside over the test without having had the opportunity to watch someone else first proctor the exam.

However to uphold the respect and dignity of my administrators and the FCAT itself, I determined to take full responsibility for my failure and if necessary be the fall guy. After all, I never desired to teach a second year anyhow. The first year had been painful enough. Yet I knew many of the administrators and faculty in the principal's office with me were career educators. I didn't want to jeopardize or harm them in any way.

Hence there truly is a time to keep your mouth shut and swallow your pride. Sometimes playing dumb (or admitting your failures and stupidity) can be the smartest thing to do.

Conversely, defending yourself can only invite more blows from the powerful hammer presiding over you. I chose to minimize the impact of the hammer's blow by remaining as silent as possible, rather than provide a posture of defiant opposition.

In moments like this you might be best served by picturing what you are going to do during your summer vacation (one of the best things about teaching).

How about a gorgeous cruise leaving Star Island (Miami, Florida) in route to the breathtaking Caribbean to forget about your woes and sorrows!

http://click.linksynergy.com/fs-bin/click?id=3RWH2TJD1YU&offerid=136622.10001179&type=3&subid=0

Paul & Isai with precious children from the village within the war-torn nation of Burundi bordering Rwanda.

Paul at Cocoa Beach near Patrick's Air Force base, one of his favorite nearby surf spots. The waves aren't all that big, but when the surf is up you can get some fun rides.

65. Agree With Your Adversary

When I was brought into my principal's office and heard her first words. "I can't believe...." I immediately and gently replied (with head down in shame), "I agree with you."

Being trained in negotiations and conflict resolution, I was somewhat interested in her reaction. To my surprise when I agreed with my principal, this somewhat diffused some of the hostility and tension in her voice.

I don't fully understand it, nor can I adequately articulate how it works. Yet I have noticed when you agree with your adversary, somehow it forges a bond and eliminates the posturing as opponents. Once you have agreed with your adversary, the need to doggedly drive home a point is no longer necessary. Now the person (in this case my principal) was brought to the next step in dealing with the problem, addressing it, and coming to a meeting of the minds as to how we would proceed.

Therefore by agreeing with your adversary (and biting the bullet in this instance for me), you are able to move on to more important things – truly solving the problem and proceeding properly into the future.

On the other hand, for those who take a more self-righteous posturing and seek to defend themselves, they can expect whatever they resist to persist. It has been my experience that educators (particularly educational administrators) like to be right and don't hold back in pursuing this objective (and making you aware of their hierarchal position in the chain of command) along the way.

I therefore am glad I took the more humble route of admitting the error of my ways and taking the discipline I was due. Had I done otherwise (as I'm sure others have done), I very well might have lost my job that day.

Pride and defending yourself can sometimes be the worst career decision you ever made. Agreeing with your adversary however can save the day.

Paul relaxing after a good meal and show on a delightful cruise.

If you'd like to sink your teeth into a delicious lobster, get one delivered straight to your kitchen!
http://www.kqzyfj.com/click-3186940-10639565

How about authentic Italian cuisine from Florence or Sicily, which will make even Olive Garden & Carrabas cry for mercy!
http://www.dpbolvw.net/click-3186940-10647162

66. Document Everything

When working with children and young adults beneath the age of eighteen, you can never be too careful and cautious. If ever something seems problematic or potentially litigious, show due diligence and thoroughly document it.

Beware of being too casual and relaxed around your students. Keep your hands to yourself and carefully select your words in an attempt to always honor and uphold every student's personal dignity.

What you may think to be an encouraging tap on the shoulder may be taken by your student to be an invasion of their personal space. Likewise a verbal reprimand may be perceived as embarrassing to a student.

Don't be afraid or fearful of being loving and warm toward your students. But do be aware that it only takes one incident to open the doors of scrutiny amid a student accusation of misconduct on your part.

Therefore be extra cautious and deliberate about your documentation, quoting students who witnessed any misbehavior in your classroom. You always want to have some eyewitnesses (even if just other students) who can back you up and verify what you are saying or writing is true. I therefore try to quote other students' reaction and characterization to misbehavior when writing my discipline referrals.

Documentation the day of the incident is always better than documentation done in retrospect days and weeks later when the incident is not as easily remembered in full.

At the high school where I worked, after calling for a dean to remove an unruly student, our teachers were required to complete a discipline referral. The discipline referral documented the incident thoroughly and remained on file to be shown to the student's parents.

Such documentation will alleviate many lawsuits, flawed and fabricated accusations, and help to reveal underlying motivations driving unruly students to disrupt your class.

Paul with Pakistani young men in Faisalabad, where he led a youth empowerment conference to raise up leaders in the nation. Paul traveled to Pakistan twice after 9-11 and was greatly impressed with their passion and professionalism.

Paul in Manchester, UK on a cool summer day with a monstrous statue of a former queen. Many Pakistanis and Indians have immigrated to England to live and work.

67. Protect Your Students' Space & Privacy

Protect your students' space and privacy to the best of your ability. In my ESOL class, we had limited space within our small classroom. I therefore had to ask all students to take their purses and bags off of the tables so each student would have adequate space to read from their books and write.

Some students were slow to obey. Therefore I asked repeatedly until my request was followed. Some students liked to hide food in their bags and try to sneakily eat in my class. Others would try to text message their friends, while hiding their cell phones in their bags.

Eventually my students realized that I had caught on to their tactics and began to come to class with the intent to work. Yet they had to be continually reminded, lest the students aimlessly wander back into the humdrum and lackluster mindset about learning English many of them came with upon arriving with their parents to the United States.

I therefore employed my motivational speaking techniques to keep audiences fully engaged and active throughout the presentation. I walked around the room and used humor where appropriate to drive home a point. By intertwining points and illustrations, I was able to awaken my students' understanding and provide helpful illumination on any given topic.

Yet whenever I walked to the back of the classroom and went behind some of the students' chairs, some began to feel a bit uncomfortable. This undoubtedly is a usual response as I myself get a bit curious and feel somewhat uncomfortable whenever a student walks behind my desk.

None of us like to encounter the unknown and be made to feel uncomfortable by someone standing behind us. I therefore tried to keep a sufficient and adequate distance between my students in the back of the room whenever I walked in their vicinity.

Allowing every student and teacher sufficient space serves us all, while making us individually and collectively feel more comfortable with one another.

Paul igniting faith and hope in the hearts of children across India, where he has traveled throughout and visited five times thus far in his young life. India shall soon surpass China becoming the world's largest populace on earth.

Paul in lovely Maldives in the Indian Ocean.

68. Join the Teachers Union

Although I did not join the teachers union for financial reasons, I recommend all career educators do. The summer before I began teaching, my car was hit and totaled by a drunk driver. Beyond my car, I sustained some serious injuries causing me a major financial setback. I therefore never joined the teachers union.

My mom certainly recommends joining the teachers union for legal and financial reasons. Considering the low salaries teachers make, why jeopardize having to defend yourself in a lawsuit were a student's parents to sue you?

America is an extremely litigious society and people don't hesitate to use the legal system to make a buck. Given the seriousness of protecting students' rights and safety in the classroom, allegations are often perceived and assumed to be accurate until proven otherwise in court.

As women typically have a bit more sympathy in court when giving testimony against their husbands, so too do students in comparison with their teachers. Unlike the old days when I was in high school, students nowadays are no longer allowed to be paddled or physically disciplined by public school faculty and staff.

Therefore the courts deal very stringently with these matters to ensure the integrity, decency, and rights of students are upheld within the educational system. That being said, a teachers union steps in to defend educators who get accused of impropriety and abuse of students.

Furthermore teachers unions have financial advice and numerous resources to empower teachers. Teachers unions provide networking opportunities with other educators and provide you a professional forum where you can speak with other educators just like you, who have similar struggles and successes to share.

Paul and his brother Franklin skiing in upstate New York.

Paul in Maui, Hawaii with a submarine behind him surfacing.

69. Be Quick to Hear & Slow to Speak

Whenever I attended staff and in-service meetings with my administration, I always endeavored to speak as little as possible and earnestly listen to learn. This approach served me well and kept me in good graces with my administrators.

I only spoke up when I needed clarification and had a question needing to be answered. I opted to avoid trying to be funny and cute (although I can be both of these as well as charming – of course I am a bit biased).

The school where I worked showcased some huge egos both in administration and among my fellow teachers. I therefore opted to be the silent type and play dumb rather than overly assert myself and get beat down.

Sometimes playing dumb is the smartest thing you can do to avoid being assigned extra work and not welcome opposition from the know-it-alls and big egos.

Plus by listening more than you speak, you learn a lot more. Certainly there is a good reason God attached two ears to our heads and made it so they always remain open, whereas our mouths have the ability to be shut. This is sufficient notice and forewarning to me as to what I am to do when surrounded by seniority, advisors, and administrators.

I particularly don't like being the noisy nail that welcomes the harsh blow of the hammer. I would far rather lay low and minimize my personal hardship. Keeping a low profile early on made my first year teaching far easier.

Paul in Las Vegas with Elvis and Marilyn Monroe in front of the famous Bellagio Hotel.

http://click.linksynergy.com/fs-bin/click?id=3RWH2TJD1YU&offerid=136622.10001435&subid=0&type=4

Treat your teachers to some fun and recreation! If you'd like Paul to arrange a spectacular getaway trip to show the teachers at your school some love and appreciation, just write Paul, tell him your budget, and suggest what you have in mind.

Whether it's Orlando, Vegas, Hawaii, or a cruise; let Paul arrange exciting travel getaways and provide professional enrichment to teachers and educational administrators.

Why not dip into your professional development budget and treat your staff to a well-needed enrichment seminar in a fabulous destination they can enjoy? They will love you for it and stick around another 5 to 10 years because you showed them you actually care about them beyond just using them as tools to serve your professional career aspirations.

70. Be Willing to Relocate to Another School

One of the bargaining chips educators have is the possibility of relocating to other schools in each county and various school boards across the country. A teacher should never feel bound or obligated to remain in a school, wherein they are unhappy. Work for a school that you find most suitable to your professional needs and compatible to your personal life.

Go where you are celebrated and happily leave where you are just being tolerated. There are schools throughout the world that would be delighted to have you teaching for them and where the students will respect you.

If you are disillusioned with teaching in North America, but know that teaching is your calling, write me to discover teaching opportunities abroad. Presently I am recruiting teachers to work in government schools located in both Japan and Korea.

The position provides you roundtrip airfare, a furnished apartment, a monthly salary of approximately $2,500 a month, and health insurance coverage. If interested email me at RevivingNations@yahoo.com and write in the subject heading "Teacher for Overseas".

Living and working abroad is a life-changing adventure that will forever enrich you, while providing you an unforgettable experience of a lifetime. If my wife would live overseas, I would go to a different country every year to teach. If she ever leaves me (which I don't want), that is my plan.

One of my goals is to touch every country on earth and empower people throughout the planet to live their dreams. It saddens me to see teachers miserable at the school where they currently teach. Yet many won't leave because they feel they have no other options. Nothing is further from the truth.

If you are willing to spread your wings and remove your limitations, there are children and school administrators throughout the globe that would be delighted to have you teach for them.

Forget your fears and follow your passion! Live your dreams and take immediate action!

Contact me today to begin living your dreams and be treated with the love and respect you deserve. Smart and career savvy educators go where they are celebrated and never linger around where they are merely tolerated.

Fly the coop, leave the compound, and live free!

Karla & Paul in front of a huge Christmas tree on Royal Caribbean's *Adventure of the Seas* cruise ship.

71. Touch a Heart Before Asking for a Hand

The best administrators know how to touch a heart and make a friend before asking for a hand. Pastors and directors of nonprofit organizations are equally skilled at this given the amount of volunteer workers they must continually recruit.

As a teacher you will be given countless opportunities to get involved and serve in innumerable capacities. If you have the stamina, desire and wherewithal by all means give yourself to whatever you are passionate about.

As for myself, my first year teaching was challenging enough given all of the required continuing education and professional exams I had to take en route to obtaining my teaching certificate. Therefore the last thing in the world I wanted to do was pile on more work, even if it was volunteer work.

I therefore never replied (and sometimes never even opened to avoid feeling guilty) to many emails soliciting help for school fundraisers and events. I know many teachers and staff probably helped out throughout the year, but I was just unable to do so.

I was embroiled in a battle against my insurance company and the drunk driver who totaled my car, leaving my family without a vehicle for nearly five months. It's hard to believe in retrospect I actually used a rental car for five months, but with gas prices at $4 a gallon during the middle of 2008, it was extremely difficult to find a replacement vehicle for my 1997 Honda Accord special edition.

It seemed every time we found a vehicle we liked, it either had mechanical issues (later revealed by our trustworthy mechanic who advised us not to buy it) or was beyond our price range. After a long ordeal and five months of waiting, we finally managed to get financing for a 2006 Hyundai Sonata, which we surprisingly purchased for $12,300 at 0% APR (a miracle of God after much prayer and patience).

Given my financial situation after the car accident, which left me in a downward tailspin, it truly was a miracle when this Christian car dealer showed up with a vehicle exactly the same as the rental car we had been driving (minus the XM radio which I really love – especially CSPAN, CNN, MSNBC, and a few other news channels).

By God's grace we got basically the same car we had driven as a rental for two months, which included the sunroof, leather interior and dual exhaust.

Perhaps my pitiful cries to my Creator eventually prevailed and God above had mercy on us giving us a car after our long ordeal. My wife Karla and I often fought over sharing a car during the first year of our marriage, but having to go back to the rental car company and get a new rental every week was unbearable.

As a teacher I urge you to be wise in what you say yes to, as for me success was determined by what I said no to. Should you lead or launch a student club or organization, remember to touch a heart before you ask for a hand.

Unconditionally love people by taking a genuine interest in them regardless if they commit to help you or not. This is one thing perhaps my administrators could have done a bit better. There was a lack of nurturing I felt among my administrators, who seemingly sought to simply get the job done rather than see how I was doing as a new teacher.

Thankfully I found some patient and tender loving care from a senior ESL teacher, who endured my questions and patiently helped me figure out the school's operating system on my computer. Had it not been for her, I would have been sunk.

That being said, remember to express your gratitude and thanks for those who take time to uphold and empower you to be successful. After all, success has many fathers and mothers. Failure however is always an orphan. Truly we all do need one another.

72. Prepare Adequately Daily

In this instance, I am encouraging you to prepare adequately daily, but perhaps don't follow in my footsteps. Since I am a more creative type and a writer, I found it a bit easier in this regard to find meaningful lessons from my two textbooks. Of course the lessons in and of themselves (literature specifically, written often hundreds of years ago, was a bit boring for my ESL students) needed a teacher to breathe life into them and animate them a bit to captivate students' interest.

I therefore prepared my lessons before class daily upon arriving at school in the morning. As an author, I do my best work and writing early in the morning when I am fresh and my surroundings are quiet.

Other teachers opted to prepare their lessons after students left school in preparation for the next day. This is the ideal way to plan and prepare lessons. I however was too exhausted and worn out by the end of each day to think straight enough to prepare meaningful lessons.

I therefore tried to arrive early to school in the morning when I could prepare the lessons. This was simply a matter of preference for me and one I'm sure many would disagree with me preferring to prepare a bit more in advance.

If you are a procrastinator or often running late, I suggest preparing a day or two beforehand to alleviate any unwanted stress or strain.

Another great way to get ideas for lesson plans is to ask other teachers more senior than yourself within your department. Some will be flattered that you were humble enough to ask (others may not respond). Other teachers may be a bit more territorial and protective of their intellectual property. Nevertheless you never know unless you ask.

Why reinvent the wheel if what you are looking for already exists. There are also many wonderful teaching resources online to help you as an educator prepare each day and wow your students.

This incredible resource for old newspaper archives below enables you to access vintage sports, war, historical, and Hollywood documents and clippings. This is a fabulous tool below for educators as they even reproduce old newspapers for you!

http://click.linksynergy.com/fs-bin/click?id=3RWH2TJD1YU&offerid=171450.10000234&subid=0&type=4

Kids come alive in class when you show them images and visuals from historical times. The untold moments in sports are incredible! Access war stories few history books ever tell in full. Give your students a full picture with unprecedented background knowledge to enliven your classroom discussions.

Help your students prepare for the SAT, LSAT, GMAT and GRE. Get your students free help on the SAT here below:
http://click.linksynergy.com/fs-bin/click?id=3RWH2TJD1YU&offerid=172326.10000056&type=3&subid=0

Compare the ACT vs. the SAT exam.
http://click.linksynergy.com/fs-bin/click?id=3RWH2TJD1YU&offerid=172326.10000059&type=3&subid=0

Make it fun by evaluating celebrity SAT scores.
http://click.linksynergy.com/fs-bin/click?id=3RWH2TJD1YU&offerid=172326.10000067&type=3&subid=0

Free practice tests with Kaplan are helpful.
http://click.linksynergy.com/fs-bin/click?id=3RWH2TJD1YU&offerid=147373.10002952&type=3&subid=0

73. Be Creative and Insightful in Your Lessons

Go with the inspirational flow whenever you teach. Textbooks are nice and a good place to begin, but ultimately trust your instincts when you are present with your students since you best know their educational needs.

Don't fear deviating from the textbook a bit whenever you feel you need to in order to further teach a topic and achieve a greater level of comprehension among students. What good is it to blaze through a topic or subject, only to leave over half of your students behind?

Utilize your creativity and ingenuity to communicate thoroughly to every student within your classroom. Rethinking and rephrasing your lessons in such a way to increase the understanding of all your students will sometimes be your greatest challenge. Finding ways to make the material interesting and relevant to your students is another ongoing challenge, but this is why you have been hired.

Without you to breathe life into the curriculum, students could droll through a boring computer screen if education was meant to just fulfill an assignment. On the contrary, kids need love and life within their educational experience. Hence you have been chosen to bring and impart that life within all you say and do.

Creativity therefore is something you must cultivate and embrace throughout your entire life, being always mindful of how you can incorporate what you are learning in your own life into your students' lessons. As you embrace being a lifelong learner, you and your students can grow together.

This is when you as an educator will begin to simultaneously mature and grow along with your students – in different ways of course, but nevertheless together cooperatively you will experience metamorphosis. Suddenly, surprisingly, and serendipitously it shall occur.

Sometimes profound revelations come out of nowhere like popcorn exploding forth within you. Other times it will be a progressive pursuit of a body of knowledge, discipline, or understanding that will culminate in a brilliant new insight which you as an educator will discover to improve your performance.

Never be intimidated by creativity or the use of your imagination to bring your lessons to life. Every teacher has a different level of creativity. Be free to explore your own ideas, thoughts, and feelings. As you do, creative breakthroughs shall flow through you!

Consider some educational toys if you are teaching younger learners.

http://click.linksynergy.com/fs-bin/click?id=3RWH2TJD1YU&offerid=167165.10000035&type=4&subid=0

Kinesthetic and visual learners always benefit from an educational experience. Instructional lectures alone never actively engage young learners to interact with the learning material. Make learning fun and memorable for kids!

Paul in Istanbul, Turkey enjoying some lamb and local cuisine.

74. Provide Lively Presentations & Lectures

If there is one thing I can do is provide lively presentations and lectures. Somehow I have the ability to take boring material and extract something interesting from it to bring it to life for my students.

Ironically, I actually abhorred and despised literature when I was in high school. My younger brother always said he wanted to teach English. Yet after all of my world travels and living abroad, where I discovered and fell into teaching English to international students, when I came home to the States this became my occupation for a while.

The extent with which international students are bored with literature written hundreds of years ago is indescribable. Nevertheless my principal told me teaching the high school English curriculum to ESL students, was required by the school board and the department of education within our county.

Therefore like a soldier under command, I wholeheartedly complied. Nevertheless I had my challenges, but inwardly I often laughed at my ability to take international students (who initially resisted using this thick literature book with very few pictures) and get them interested in the pearls found within literature and various English forms of expression.

Enthusiasm undeniably is contagious. Just think in your own life how often you bought something you weren't interested in and didn't need simply because the sales person's enthusiasm was contagious.

Likewise as an educator your enthusiasm is equally contagious and dangerous. The danger exists when you come to class off your mark, dull, and weary in well doing. If you cannot pull yourself together (and be a bit of an actor or actress) and fake it until you make it, your students will feel the same disinterest in their studies that you their teacher feel toward presenting the material.

I have found it is far better (and a more efficient use of an educator's energy) to pull yourself together and muster the energy to attract your students interest in the learning material than to lose your students by way of disinterest and have to play the disciplinarian the entire class to keep your kids on task.

Paul in Washington D.C. at a historical institute & museum.

75. Provide Meaningful Group Work for Students

Sometimes the most beneficial thing a teacher can do for his or her students is to facilitate meaningful interactive group work, wherein students can use the material they have been taught in conversation and real life exercises.

As an ESL teacher, I enjoy facilitating dialogue and meaningful interaction for my students. It allows me to monitor and watch their use of the language. Often I can gauge and determine a learner's language level based on their verbal communication and written work.

By no means does a student's grade level reveal their language level. Within the state of Florida, students cannot be failed for not mastering the English language. That being said, ESL students are given upon request bilingual dictionaries to assist them in test taking.

Studying English as a foreign language and taking your entire school course work in a second language is doubly challenging. ESL students therefore are amazingly gifted and intensely committed to be able to endure this level of academic coursework.

Imagine if you a native English speaker were made to relocate to China, where you were told to learn Mandarin and simultaneously given all of your coursework in Mandarin. How well do you think you would perform academically?

This scenario is often no different for Latino and Haitian students immigrating with their parents to the United States. When these transplanted students (who have come here to accompany their parents, many not overly exuberant to say the least) are made to learn a second language and an entire curriculum within that second language, is it any wonder they sometimes get discouraged and feel overwhelmed?

I know I certainly felt overwhelmed when I lived in Taipei, Taiwan for six months and had to learn a few words and phrases in Mandarin just to survive daily. I cannot fathom the extent of the difficulty it would be to learn a new language, while learning all of your school subjects in that new language.

Group work for me as an ESL teacher allowed my students with different language levels to interact and help each other out along the way. Given the steep learning curve for some newly immigrated students just beginning to become familiar with English, the group activities helped immensely and enabled students to cooperatively work together.

Group activities can be very useful to bridge the gap within education and minimize the amount of intimidation a struggling student feels in the classroom. No matter what subject you're teaching, some amount of group work makes learning meaningful to students as they interact among themselves and become familiar with the material in their own way.

Paul with children at a school he visited and spoke at in Mumbai, India. Some of the world's brightest minds come from India to study in Universities across North America every year.

Paul was certainly impressed with the discipline and mastery of English among the children at this school, where he was happily welcomed by these bright-eyed youngsters.

76. Help Out Whenever and Wherever You Can

A sure way to gain the favor and good graces of your administrators and senior teachers at your school is to volunteer to help any way you can. Everybody loves someone with a servant's heart and hand to help.

You therefore can curry favor and get in the inner circle with the powers that be at your school by serving. I highly suggest serving willingly from the heart, expecting nothing in return. When you serve with strings attached, even if unspoken and inwardly expecting something in return, others will perceive and feel it.

It is best to be real, sincere, and serve because you genuinely want to help. Over time as you show yourself likeable, trustworthy, helpful, and dependable it is very likely you will be asked to do more – or given more responsibility.

If you like this sort of thing and desire to work as an administrator one day, then this would be a wise career move for you to pursue. Just be forewarned that when hired and serving as a teacher, that is your first priority and order of business.

The last thing you want to do is let your teaching begin to suffer because of all of your other extracurricular projects and volunteer tasks you are attending to.

Help out with a smile and be willing to get your hands dirty. Such a team player will never lack for a job, nor will your administrators ever want to get rid of you when jobs cuts start happening due to economic constraints.

Honestly, I cannot say I have excelled at serving given my peculiar and overwhelming circumstances in which I was entangled after suffering a grueling car accident wherein I suffered physically and financially. Nevertheless what I came to see while teaching again revealed to me this universal truth as to the power of serving.

Serving those around you, no matter their status or position will usually without fail endear them to you and progressively cause you to gain their trust and favor.

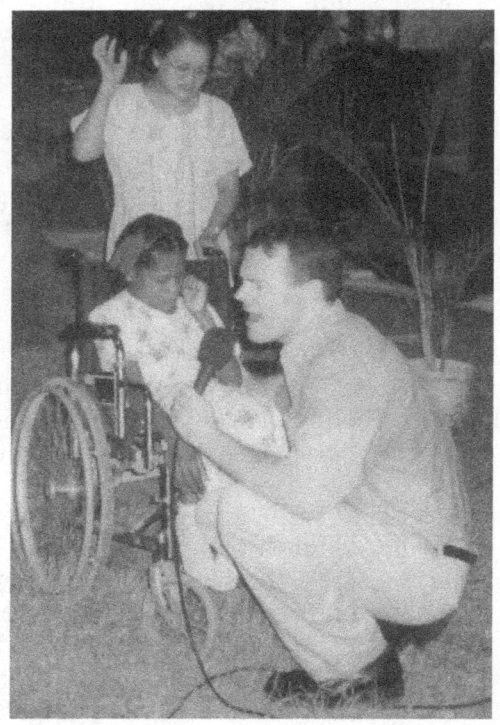

Paul praying for a precious little girl in Guyana.

Give your students a global perspective by listening to international radio broadcasts, some of the best on the web.

http://click.linksynergy.com/fs-bin/click?id=3RWH2TJD1YU&offerid=129871.10000055&type=3&subid=0

77. Don't Ever Be Alone with A Student

Beware and take necessary precautions whenever it looks like you might be alone with a student. Sit in the library together or at the cafeteria. Whenever you're alone with a student, meet in a public place to avoid the appearance of evil and any accusations that might arise from onlookers.

Be wise and prudent, foreseeing the potential pitfalls that could short circuit and trip up your professional career. You've worked far too hard as an educator to jeopardize your future by putting yourself in a precarious situation that might injure or damage your reputation.

Even if you don't have eyes for a student, you never know when they may have eyes for you. If they do, it is likely the student has told their friends about their feelings for you. This means you often are the last one to find out. Therefore if you see anything that looks suspicious or smells fishy, go with your instincts immediately and guard yourself.

Teachers make far too little in their salary to have to deal with a sexual harassment lawsuit from a student's parent. Moreover with the extent of frivolous lawsuits being commenced by litigious and money hungry people, you can never be too safe as an educator.

Besides guilt often does not need to be proven if the appearance of wrongdoing exists. Appearances and accusations are often sufficient to scare and threaten any school board to pay up before having to go to court and suffer a lack of public trust as a result of a pending lawsuit.

Courts and juries typically side with and believe children and young adults before giving ear to what a teacher may have to say about the situation. Therefore be safe early on to avoid costly litigation and getting laid off down the road for lack of foresight and discernment.

Near the end of my first year teaching, I received an email from a national board certified teacher who was the point man on campus from the teachers' union. He informed me that anybody who wanted to add their own personal comments to their principal's professional evaluation on file was legally permitted and authorized to do so.

Most new teachers probably don't think to do so, but I highly recommend it. Nobody can characterize your time teaching better than you. Principals and administrators have a far different perspective, as they are not in the classroom teaching everyday. Their focus is very often entirely different.

Therefore when you feel it is appropriate and needed to provide additional information to more accurately detail your experience as an educator, don't hesitate to take the initiative to add this to your file.

Check with your state's department of education to be sure of the professional evaluation protocol and your legal rights. Never should you let your principal have the only and final word on you. If there is something negative or questionable in your file, speak up and add your comments.

While doing bus duty one afternoon after the dismissal of my students from school, I spoke with a fellow teacher who had a pending lawsuit filed against her. Given the fact she was an ESE (exceptional student educator) I was a bit shocked. She explained the lawsuit was over her IEP (individual education plan) for the student in question.

Apparently the parents disagreed with an aspect of the IEP and decided to file a lawsuit to see that it was changed. As en educator, you can never be too careful. Considering the minimal amount of money you earn as an educator, always exercise due diligence when dealing with your students. Even when you have given all of your heart and energy to do everything right, you still may occasionally get a lawsuit or complaint filed against you. Therefore document everything and be as detailed as possible lest you forget later.

78. Cultivate Humility Professionally & Personally

Humility will always serve you well and usually precede honor and wealth. Somehow humility brings the favor of God and others to your life. By being humble and tenderhearted enough to listen and be a lifelong learner, people will trust and respect you.

Avoid the tendency to be a know-it-all and show off. Genuinely listen to and learn from people, even if you feel like you already know what they are saying to you. By showing humility, you will learn far more than you thought and further solidify those vital truths within your own heart by hearing the matter again.

Humility will surprisingly promote you as people relate more to transparency than perfection. Educational administrators like people they can trust. Trustworthy people are far more valuable and easy to work with than know-it-alls who cannot admit when they mess up.

Avoid the tendency to become coldhearted and grow rigid and frigid in your ways. Let humility guard your heart, keep you forever learning, empower you to be strong, and continually produce personal growth within you. Truly humility will hasten your next promotion.

Even when there is no promotion for you in the horizon, humility will endear people to you and develop a greater level of trust among those near you.

As a personal rule, I have decided to love and respect everyone (even when they may not love and respect me). This is because I believe everybody deeply yearns to be loved and affirmed. Plus I truly believe some aspect of every human being's life has something to give, contribute, and teach us if we will take time to observe and listen.

When you die to your ego and the need to be right, you will transcend the tendency to be self-righteous and more quickly reconcile with those around about you making your life far better. A meaningful life is one in which you connect well with others. Although you may not fully (or even partially in some instances) agree with people, you can peaceably and respectfully interact with them.

By doing so you show yourself to be agreeable and likeable. Never let politics, religion, ideological persuasions, or your educational philosophy erect walls and alienate others from being able to interact with you at a relational level.

Make it your aim to win friends rather than create more enemies daily. If you can learn to connect better with others, be more socially in touch, and genuinely care about people; your life will flourish magnificently far beyond your professional capacities.

Life is larger than you, your work, and accomplishments. When you allow others to live and simply be without your judgments and criticisms, you cause life to be far more pleasant in the workplace.

Cultivate harmonious relationships by finding the mutual place of agreement in all things. Surely everybody has a point of agreement. It may be as simple as admiring the weather, laughing about a common problem we all face, or rejoicing in a season of life every human being goes through. Find the place of agreement and learn to get along with people.

Rejoice with they who are in a season of rejoicing and comfort those enduring seasons of suffering. By doing so you will show yourself to be empathetic, agreeable, and likeable.

Passion flows from connecting with people, not merely being professional and pompous. Love people more than your profession and your profession will always be enlivened with heartfelt inspiration.

Be gracious, kind, and complimentary. It will lighten the emotional load for people and brighten their day.

79. Beware of Know-It-Alls and Big Egos.

I like the movie *Forest Gump* and recall the scene wherein he says, "I'm not a smart man." Although Forest seemingly was not a smart man according to his own confession, I felt he was rather emotionally intelligent.

Forest knew he loved Jenny and thought they were meant to be together like peas and carrots. Within the educational system and schools in particular, not every educator works well together. Some frankly will be like sandpaper and continually rub you the wrong way.

One seasoned educator (probably nearing her retirement) nearby me often asked questions, which sometimes were a bit loaded and rhetorical. I often smiled, found a way of escape, and withdrew from any possible professionally damaging conversations (as I didn't really know, nor feel comfortable with her ...realizing if somebody will gossip with me, they will thereafter likely gossip to others about me).

Hence hopping on board with know-it-alls is often an accident waiting to happen. Unless you like throwing yourself under the bus, beware of nosey teachers who like to stir up trouble and probe into matters not concerning them.

On the surface what they say may seem somewhat alright, but inwardly you will feel the devilish undercurrent salivating for little morsels of information to later do you harm. Whenever you feel this alerting red flag in your spirit, listen to it and remove yourself from such a person. Your gut within is often far more intuitive and intelligent than your head atop your shoulders.

Nobody likes people with big egos who act like know-it-alls. Usually such personalities are deeply insecure, selfish, and poor listeners. Big egos attract attack and opposition, as they awaken the pride in us all to try to outdo them and stand tall. Don't fall into the empty trap of pursuing what exalts you and puffs up your ego. Because after your ego is fed, you will be left feeling empty inside.

Incidentally, this teacher next door liked to borrow stuff of mine, which later I had to hunt for to get returned. I don' t like or appreciate this sort of thing, as I believe when you borrow something you should take the initiative to return it yourself.

Big egos are often condescending. One afternoon after questioning a dean on staff about something via email, I received an email from my principal answering my question. Upon scrolling down further I noticed the dean had written about me to the principal saying, "Is he confused?"

I was by no means confused. I just had sought clarification on a matter pertaining to student award ceremonies. Unlike most teachers, my classes were mixed with students from several grade levels.

Therefore the usual mass email with attached instructions didn't perfectly fit my situation. Upon inquiring my dean seemingly got more confused herself and not knowing how to reply just forwarded it on to my principal (something that rarely serves you well as a teacher).

Thankfully my principal was a bit more knowledgeable about my situation and graciously answered the question. Condescending answers and belittling fellow coworkers (even when they are leaving, as I was at the end of the year) is never a good thing to do. (Besides you never know when they might write a book about you.)

Overall however this dean was really a phenomenal person and actually covered for me the same week when I had to get a substitute to replace me when I was ill. The dean kindly submitted the request for the substitute for me and pulled one of my earlier prepared "emergency" lesson plans for the sub. Truly staying humble, holding your tongue, and being thankful does serve you better professionally and when you are in need.

80. Lose Some Battles to Win the War.

You can never please everyone. I heard the legendary comedian Bill Cosby say a long time ago, "I don't know the secret to success, but a sure way to failure is to try to please everybody."

The same is true in any profession and certainly for an educator. Teachers sometimes are like little hens, given to nitpicking and pecking at each other in the employee break room and dining hall during lunch. Some teachers make a meal of their principal and administrators for lunch, rather than going to the cafeteria for bodily nourishment. Gossip spreads like wildfire and soon gets distorted beyond measure to the extent that little truth remains afterward.

Therefore don't believe everything you hear through the grapevine, because those grapes may be sour and set your teeth on edge and sicken your stomach.

It is far better to humble yourself, admit to any questionable wrong doing, seek clarification as to how you can do better, and keep a pure heart always ready to improve and make any necessary adjustments.

Seek to be reconciled before seeking to be right. The teachers who seek to be right and privately endeavor to voice their opinions rarely have any influence to begin with. This is why they whisper and gossip in a corner, rather than publicly speaking to the principal or administrators face to face.

Eventually your words will catch up to you and your motives expose you. Therefore cultivate a pure heart, believe the best about people, and be gracious. We all need a dose of mercy and grace once in a while. Also remember you never know the extent of a teacher or administrator's personal problems and challenges occurring privately beyond the four walls of the school. Therefore be kind and tenderhearted before slandering someone unnecessarily.

It is far better to withhold premature judgment than to speak hastily erroneously and presumptuously, only to later have to apologize and seek to make amends. Reconciling after an injustice or unkind word has been spoken is far more difficult than just keeping quiet in the first place.

Before you give somebody a piece of your mind, try giving him or her a piece of your heart. That approach will make your life far more sweet and your profession significantly more enjoyable.

Whenever you give someone a piece of your heart it feels better from the start. Besides your heart is far more powerful than your head. Therefore if you want to get ahead, use your heart more than your head.

When your head cannot figure something out and people are annoying you beyond measure, revert back to listening to your heart and discover the right thing to do in any given situation.

Being reconciled and hugging is far more fulfilling for me within my marriage than fighting, which is the least productive course of action and utterly exhausting emotionally.

Therefore sometimes the most intelligent thing you can do is to lose the battle so you can maintain your focus to win the larger war at hand.

When doing so, be sure not to tell the other person what you are doing lest they resurrect the incident and altercation all over again to begin a whole new fight.

As for me, I prefer being a lover rather than a fighter. It is far more fun loving rather than fighting. When you fight you are always going to get hurt in some way, even if not today you can be sure eventually as old wounds between rivals don't die easy. Therefore to make your life easier, swallow your pride and be willing to lose a battle or two to ensure long-term victory.

81. Be Merciful and Hopeful for Change.

Kids can be cruel no matter what their age may be. It doesn't take long to discover the cruelty and lack of hesitation with which your students will cut each other and you down. Without a moment's notice of forewarning, you can quickly be degraded right before your entire class.

When I had a cold sore on my mouth one week, a particularly student who had been a discipline problem the entire year began saying, "I'm glad I don't have herpes!"

Thankfully because I paid him no attention, most of my students didn't either. Moreover many of my ESL students didn't even register the word. Nevertheless my little devil made his point. I however didn't add any fuel to the fire by disregarding his remarks and thereby was able to direct the attention of my class on to more meaningful things such as completing their presentation. That day my little devil came forward and gave two presentations (at two different times) rather than just the required one making him an overachiever.

I therefore gave him extra credit, which made him very happy. Overcome evil with good whenever you can, because focusing on negativity never lifts anybody out of it.

Instead of cursing the darkness, light a candle and shine bright. As you do others will awaken in the midst of your illumination and happily follow you. To be ensnared and entangled in darkness is never fun, neither is talking about it. Be the light of your classroom and the thermometer that sets the temperature. The atmosphere in which you teach and lead your students is yours to govern. Don't get sidetracked by your ego and become emotionally embroiled. Possess your soul with patience and hold on to the reins of power within your classroom. Overcome evil with good and transform devils into angels.

When your little darlings turn into devils for the day, always remain hopeful, knowing that you yourself have not always been a little angel. Hope is an anchor to stabilize your soul and enable you to walk by faith not by sight. See beyond the present circumstance you are now facing so you can cultivate and develop the future of your students. Speak to their potential and pull them beyond their present.

I was successfully able to do this when one of my problematic students and I began to have difficulties in class. After giving the class their daily assignment, I took time away from grading papers long enough to sit down alongside this student and express my expectations for him.

During my heart-to-heart talk with the student I said, "Marvin, you're a great young man with enormous potential. The only problem is sometimes you are a bit rude and disruptive. If you can't get your way, instead of doing what is best for everybody, you explode and co crazy. If you could just stay calm and seek understanding before blowing up, you could do so much better and maintain the high regard everybody has toward you."

At the time I didn't know if I was getting through to him. When I assured Marvin, I wasn't his enemy, but rather his friend, I also gave him a copy of an email I had sent just weeks ago nominating him for the student of the week award. He quietly processed his misperception of me and within days our relationship as teacher-and-student completely changed for the better.

Being merciful is a mighty weapon to transform the status quo and let students know how much you care. Your ability to overlook a transgression will speak volumes as to your personal stability and ability to love unconditionally (something kids often lack at home and inwardly long for desperately).

Communicate your heartfelt faith in students and reveal to them the great potential you see they possess. Be their cheerleader even when you are seeking to discipline them and it will help bring about the transformation you desire.

82. Report Suspected Child Abuse & Neglect.

Whenever you get a whiff of possible child neglect, report it immediately to your guidance counselor and administration. Sometimes students will allude to neglect subtly.

For example one of my students told me his father refused to buy him the $20 gym clothes needed for him to workout at physical education. Therefore he failed the P.E. class because he didn't have the workout clothes required.

Upon inquiring further my administrator told me that no student is ever denied access for monetary reasons and immediately changed his grade to a passing score.

Some of my students have mentioned suicide. Even whenever the "suicide" word is said playfully or halfheartedly, I take it very seriously and immediately report it to the student's guidance counselor for follow up. Many students hurt and struggle with various issues, particular those in high school with changing hormones and fluctuating emotions. Guidance counselors provide a sympathetic ear to listen to them and have the appropriate amount of time to give proper advice.

As a teacher, trying to perform a full-fledged intervention is not only beyond your job description, but it usually is out of your area of expertise. I'm a bit privy to the ins and outs of interventions as a life coach and licensed minister. Yet as a teacher even I would not dare to be presumptuous or overstep the boundaries of my authority to which I had been given as an educator.

I gave one particular student who was obviously downcast and burdened in her heart a copy of my book *Breakthrough for a Broken Heart*, which apparently helped her quite a bit as she thanked me the next day. Her countenance definitely experienced a beautiful transformation.

Unfortunately, because of the way our schedule was structured I often had very little time between classes to speak to students. Not to mention I often needed to go to the bathroom or get ready for my next class before the bell rang. Nevertheless I always tried to give a quick word of wisdom or shared a personal story of overcoming a similar difficulty briefly in class to gently encourage the struggling student without singling them out by name.

Little by little I do believe I made a difference. Often my students would later thank me and become increasingly kind toward me.

Karla & Paul after taking in a show aboard the *Adventure of the Seas* by Royal Caribbean. If you've never gone on a cruise before, you owe it to yourself to "Get out there!"

http://click.linksynergy.com/fs-bin/click?id=3RWH2TJD1YU&offerid=136622.10000993&type=3&subid=0

Paul was skeptical for years, but after going on his first cruise was hooked and amazed at how less expensive cruising is compared to traveling the world as he used to.

Paul can sleep just about anywhere too so he hasn't ever had any problems with seasickness. The big ships knife through the big seas with little rocking and turbulence.

83. Refer Emotional Problems to the Guidance Counselors.

Once in a while as a teacher you may encounter a child or student who is troubled emotionally. This may cause them to be on edge with any form of authority and subconsciously provoke them to lash out at you whenever you seek to provide direction as an educator.

Guidance counselors have adequate and sufficient time to bring the student in and peel away the layers (usually by calmly listening and gently asking questions) to get beneath their skin to find out what really is troubling him or her.

This exchange and dialogue can be very useful and empowering for the student. Knowing they are not alone in their life's battles is very reassuring for any young person. Therefore do not hesitate to suggest a student visits their guidance counselor and to facilitate such a meeting where you deem it appropriate.

The quicker you deal with problems early on, the easier it is to solve them. When however you fail to swiftly address a problem, by reason of ignoring it the problem can grow and later escalate into something larger.

If you see a student going off course, catch and correct them early on before more harm is done. Sometimes harm done is irreversible and cannot be fixed by revisiting it. Teenage pregnancy, physical abuse, and suicide are just a few examples of what can occur when a troubled student is left to himself or herself without proper intervention.

I worked as a substitute teacher one year at Beta Center for unwed mothers finishing high school. It was heartbreaking to see some of the fine young ladies who had gotten themselves into precarious situations, many of which could have been avoided had they been properly parented or instructed at home.

Guidance counselors can often bridge and fill in the gaps if given ample forewarning and the opportunity to speak into a child's life. Pivotal times come upon us all, but no time is more paramount than that of childhood when students are most impressionable.

Once in their teenage years, students become a bit harder and less pliable. Nevertheless even teenagers desire guidance and heartfelt instruction to direct their lives for the better. Too often guidance counselors (because of principal and school board demands due to understaffing) are being used in areas beyond their expertise (or made merely to serve as laborers until trouble arises). Guidance counselors at my school informed me 90% of their job consisted of paperwork and 10% counseling (something they didn't expect when pursuing their masters degree in educational counseling). Most school guidance counselors rarely get time to eat lunch before they are being called to attend to something. What is most troubling is for all of their occupational sacrifices, guidance counselors are only compensated an extra $1.64 an hour more than teachers.

Therefore instead of waiting for the guidance counselors to take the initiative and speak to a student, as a teacher you should be their eyes and ears. That means the minute you smell trouble or see something needing to be addressed, pull that student aside and speak to them at your earliest opportunity. Thereafter refer them to the guidance counselor to go deeper and obtain additional assistance.

Since I come from a ministerial background with Biblical training in counseling, I am more apt and inclined to speak to students. Nevertheless because of the rigors and schedule demands of teaching, I rarely have the time during the day to sit and talk with a student at any length.

Occasionally my students (on their own initiative) would visit me before or after school, which I always enjoyed as I know they greatly benefited from it. However some students feel more comfortable going to somebody other than a teacher to spill their guts and share their problems. For this reason guidance counselors are a phenomenal resource on campus teachers don't call on enough. Students need somebody to confide in occasionally and should not be ashamed for doing so. It's difficult for students always having to be under and answer to authority at their age. A counseling session can enable youth to be heard, while providing enlightenment to gently change a student's perspective on a matter.

84. Encourage Career Resources & Scholarships

Every middle and high school typically has a career resource center where internships and scholarships can be applied for by deserving students. Encourage your students to visit their career counselor to learn about all of the wonderful opportunities available for them.

This is one thing I regret I never knew about growing up. Had I known then what I know now, I would have applied for study abroad programs, travel exchange semesters, internships, and scholarships.

Many wonderful opportunities and internships are available for deserving and desirous students. The White House has internships for students. The FBI and CIA also have great intern opportunities, both of which can be accessed online usually at their website. If you have difficulty finding them on the website, scroll to the bottom of the page and click on internships or careers.

Travel abroad programs provide an education far beyond what any book or course can do. My world travels taught me so much about other cultures and people, while improving my interpersonal and communication skills along the way. Such experiences will remain with me for a lifetime and are to me priceless.

A Chinese exchange student who was within my ESL program was a delight to teach. Upon arriving, he originally had my class for two hours a day. After being tested and assessed for his English language ability, this bright young man was moved out of ESL into regular English classes. He so enjoyed my class he immediately went to administration to protest and got put back into my class for an hour a day.

I certainly enjoyed having this advanced placement student. He was my only Asian student within the ESL program and the perspective he added to classroom discussions was enlightening and instructive for all of us. Nothing teaches us like interacting with the global community and gaining diverse perspectives on an issue. When we narrowly evaluate issues from our own perspective alone, we do ourselves a great disservice and tend to be a bit arrogant. Interacting with others of a different background and ideological persuasion however challenges our presumptions and keeps us sharp intellectually.

Therefore endeavor to embrace your world and live your dreams. The global community has so much to offer us all. Open your mind to a world of possibilities and do whatever you can to facilitate meaningful opportunities for your students. Create awareness and build bridges for your students to cross over into their future.

Some websites for scholarships are:

http://www.fastweb.com

http://www.scholarships.com

http://apps.collegeboard.com/cbsearch_ss/welcome.jsp

http://www.finaid.org/scholarships/

http://www.college-scholarships.com/

http://www.studentscholarshipsearch.com/

http://www.afrotc.com/scholarships/

http://www.scholarshiphelp.org/

http://www.collegescholarships.com/scholarships_apply.html

85. Promote Leisurely Reading for Pleasure

Beyond textbooks and assigned reading in class, endeavor to cultivate a love for leisurely reading material among your students. This type of reading is what nourishes your students' intellectual curiosity the most, as they proactively select and choose that which they will read based on their personal interests.

Reading for leisure and personal pleasure allows students to happily engage a body of knowledge for self-enrichment. Whether for enjoyment, entertainment, or information: such reading edifies students.

Students need to experience reading books freely on their own accord and initiative. Otherwise if reading only occurs to fulfill an assignment and obtain a grade, we will have removed the joy of reading all together leaving students feeling like reading is imprisonment and punishment.

Certainly this is not our goal as educators. Therefore share with your students what books you are currently reading for pleasure and encourage them to do likewise. Always strive and purpose to make learning an enjoyable experience.

Have your musically inclined students check out these many music magazines to choose from and get incredible discounts off normal cover prices.

http://www.magazineline.com/Haupt/Category/CategoryForm.aspx?SiteID=26&CategoryCode=MU&FormPromoSource=2&AffiliateID=LJZ-4C250&

Over 100 magazines on sale:

http://click.linksynergy.com/fs-bin/click?id=3RWH2TJD1YU&offerid=86407.10000111&type=4&subid=0

Get 50% off USA Today, the newspaper with the best photographs and daily coverage of all of the breaking news across America. Captivate your students and inspire them!
http://www.kqzyfj.com/click-3186940-4083203

Get 25% off for photo books for graduation day or something special for cultivating your students' creativity.
http://click.linksynergy.com/fs-bin/click?id=3RWH2TJD1YU&offerid=120341.10000115&type=3&subid=0

Rest your eyes and pleasure your ears! Get a 15-day trial with these incredible books for all ages on audio!
http://click.linksynergy.com/fs-bin/click?id=3RWH2TJD1YU&offerid=172119.10000074&type=3&subid=0

If you as an educator need some encouragement yourself today, try these books for all ages to inspire teachers and students to greatness! Be invigorated to conquer challenges!
http://click.linksynergy.com/fs-bin/click?id=3RWH2TJD1YU&offerid=139925.10000161&type=4&subid=0

America's premiere environmental organization, the Sierra Club, produces a wonderful magazine that will teach kids the importance of preserving our environment and give them a durable backpack for school or camping upon joining.
http://click.linksynergy.com/fs-bin/click?id=3RWH2TJD1YU&offerid=46111.10000107&type=3&subid=0

Textbooks and video games for less, a combination your students cannot refuse!
http://click.linksynergy.com/fs-bin/click?id=3RWH2TJD1YU&offerid=20738.10000028&type=4&subid=0

86. Encourage Students to Write Letters

Even better however than tying your students up solely in the books, why not release them to utilize the learning material you have taught them?

For example after teaching communication and negotiation, I taught my ESL students how to draft and write a letter of complaint. Many of my students had issues with their cell phone providers who had lied to them at the time of purchase and later revised their contracts. Several students were being charged more than they were originally told.

Another student had bought a product on Ebay that was never delivered. I taught him how to dispute the matter with his family's credit card company.

One young lady's mother had her hours reduced at work. I taught her how to write a professional and heartfelt letter to the employer asking for more hours, gently explaining the family's economic situation and needs.

A bright young man in one of my classes had a father who knew very little English and had been taken advantage of by an immigration service provider, who apparently charged him a ridiculously high fee but never produced an immigration work permit, nor any legal resident documents.

Basically this immigration intermediary company was preying on immigrants moving to the United States who did not know how to speak English. Empty promises were continually made that the documentation was being processed. Yet the delays were nothing more than a stalling tactic to buy time to hold hard earned money of sincere people trying to obey U.S. law en route to obtaining citizenship.

Therefore by teaching my students to write letters of complaint, they were empowered to be proactive rather than sit on their hands and do nothing while being taken advantage of financially.

One Mexican young man got happy and shared a story about how his father was called a "dumb Mexican" at Circuit City (a now bankrupt store). His father immediately asked to speak to the manager. Upon making a complaint against the employee, the worker was fired and the matter was resolved.

The irony of all of this is that prior to Circuit City going bankrupt, a billionaire from Mexico bought a large stake in the company to keep it afloat for a while before liquidating the company in its entirety.

The morale of the story is to always be aware of who you are calling dumb. You may get away with some mischief for a while, but eventually judgment day will come.

Among the many reflective essays I had my high school students write, some of the topics I chose were discrimination, humility, steps to success, and dream vacations.

Check out Microsoft's store below and cutting edge technology to integrate their software into your classroom. Writing assignments with the right kind of software makes learning more meaningful and teaching simple.

http://click.linksynergy.com/fs-bin/click?id=3RWH2TJD1YU&offerid=166833.10000357&subid=0&type=4

Beware of downloading stuff you are unsure of as sometimes that can destroy your operating system and trash all of your files that you worked tirelessly for years to create.

For your own personal computer's maintenance and protection, consider the following from Microsoft (a name you can trust):

http://click.linksynergy.com/fs-bin/click?id=3RWH2TJD1YU&offerid=166833.10000329&subid=0&type=4

87. Teach Students to Value & Respect Money

One of the best things you can do for your students is to teach them to value money and respect their parents who provide for them. Explain to your students that earning money doesn't come easy, but requires effort and hard work.

Once you've taught youth how to value money and not take for granted those providing for them, it is wise to teach your students to think creatively how they can render a service to earn the money they want and need.

We all have gifts, talents, and abilities. When we think of problems we can solve, we begin to engineer ways we can both serve humanity and profit handsomely. As we think along these lines we can work smarter rather harder.

I teach my students how to make money online, write a resume, interview for a job, and so much more. I also teach the importance of proper health, sufficient rest, exercise, nutrition, and detoxification of the body. These are life sustaining and survival skills that are of great value far beyond the classroom.

The United States of America is the most obese nation on earth. We're constipated and overweight. Proper nutrition, bodily maintenance, and exercise are essential to ensure optimal health and peak performance.

If we are to assimilate nutrients and adequately eliminate our food after consumption, we must modify our diets to contain more fibrous grains and fruits & vegetables. Moreover like a toilet, if we are to experience a fat flush, we must drink more water. It's difficult to flush a toilet without water. Yet we rarely drink enough water.

Caffeine filled beverages only further dehydrate the body. To replenish ourselves we need water, not sugar, salt, and caffeine. Carbonated drinks reduce bone density. Drinks stored in aluminum cans can lead to Alzheimer's disease and erode brain cells, as the aluminum seeps into the liquid.

Even bottled water, if left in the sun, can seep harmful toxins from the plastic bottle into our water and cause cancer. These are things young people need to know and be forewarned about to protect their health.

Beyond money, students must learn to value and cherish that which is priceless – their health and families. These things no amount of money can buy or replace.

Teachers in that regard need to be better examples and role models. The school where I taught was very progressive when it came to the cafeteria menu, choosing whole grains over white bread and white rice. Even our Friday pizzas had whole grain in the dough, which was a huge step forward.

Yet the teachers themselves were often obese and out of shape. Besides the coaches (who usually are more apt to being in shape as a result of being outdoors regularly) teachers also need to attend to their physical health and personal wellbeing.

School budgets for substitutes could conserve and save thousands of dollars annually if its teachers were healthier. On that note consider some of the following below to help.

For vitamins at a great price shipped for free: http://click.linksynergy.com/fs-bin/click?id=3RWH2TJD1YU&offerid=116038.10000265&type=4&subid=0

Dermatologist skin care and samples, along with a 100% money back guaranty. http://click.linksynergy.com/fs-bin/click?id=3RWH2TJD1YU&offerid=30329.10000023&type=4&subid=0

After saving your health, save money by shopping at Goodwill where you can get bundles of books for pennies each. Read the book *Toxic Relief* by Dr. Don Colbert. http://click.linksynergy.com/fs-bin/click?id=3RWH2TJD1YU&offerid=147267.10000044&type=3&subid=0

88. Teach Students How to Negotiate

Negotiation is a vital part of communication that we know too little about. Everyday in some capacity we all negotiate. Whether it is concerning who is going to do the dishes or take out the trash in our homes, the price we will pay to replace the tires on our car, the amount we will pay for a health club membership, or relationally persuading someone we have feelings for to take a mutual interest in us; all of these scenarios contain elements of negotiation.

It is useful therefore to teach students the basics about negotiation – time, information, and power. The generation in which we live is so painfully impatient that we often bulldoze over one another and explode the minute we don't get what we want. Many of these incidents escalate and become altercations requiring police intervention, which we often hear about on the local evening news.

Time within the framework of negotiation is all too important, because it is a key element by which the parties wield (or forsake) their influence and leverage (or lose) their demands.

For example if a principal is running out of time to fill a teaching position, he or she may lower the bar a bit too quickly to find someone to fill the slot. The reverse is true where there is ample time to interview several candidates for the job.

Information is what I believe to be the most important element in a negotiation. Within our culture where most people are incapable of keeping their mouths shut, it is rather easy to obtain and gather information by curiously asking the right questions. Yet revealing too much information can give your competitor a sizeable advantage once your motivations, interests, and pursuits have fully been revealed. Peculiarities pertinent to your situation once revealed give away valuable bargaining power and put you at a great disadvantage in any negotiations.

For example if your family's only car has just been totaled and you are shopping for a new car, you might not want to spill the beans and reveal this to the car salesman. Project a bit more of an emotionally detached persona, wherewith you can walk away if a good deal and fair price is not given for the car you are considering buying.

Playing with power and performing under pressure is the third element of any negotiations that is beneficial to know. Students know and understand power more than you think. Young people "mom and pop" their parents and pit them against each other cleverly to get what they want.

When dad says no to a request, sometimes kids subtly and privately go ask their mother the same request. Hoping for a different response, they sometimes get it. The result may later lead to dissension between mom and dad. Nevertheless the child may temporarily get what they want.

A wise parent however will not hastily answer their child's request affirmatively without first asking, "What did your mother (or father) say when you asked her (or him)?"

Intuitively we often navigate through the nuances of negotiation everyday. As a teacher however being able to break down the pieces of negotiation will be very enlightening and educational for your students.

If your PC or Mac is having difficulty negotiating through your network, eliminate the hassles with excellent software and components here for home or work:
http://click.linksynergy.com/fs-bin/click?id=3RWH2TJD1YU&offerid=173591.10000067&type=4&subid=0

89. Teach Conflict Resolution Techniques & Skills

Role-playing in class can be a wonderful way to teach conflict resolution techniques and communication skills. These exercises will provide students an opportunity to learn and live the lesson being imparted, which further deepens and enriches the learning experience.

For example students can be put in groups of three and given the roles of mother, father, and child. Each can role-play and act out a domestic conflict that arises at home. The child can have a temper tantrum, while the parents sort out what to do. The process can be very enlightening and instructive as students participate and observe the interaction.

Unfortunately conflict resolution and emotional management is rarely taught in our schools. Yet this is perhaps one thing our children need the most when growing up and going through the various seasons of life. Navigating through seasons of change and stages of growth can be complicated and challenging.

Understanding how to deal with unmet wants and needs can also be emotionally perplexing. Seeing other students with things that you want can also cause feelings of jealousy and envy. Dealing with cruel kids in your school can be nerve racking and make any pupil downright angry. Such emotions and feelings of hostility, if not properly discerned and managed, can further fester and reach a boiling point. Thereafter once a student is over the edge emotionally, they could explode and become confrontational. Verbal and physical confrontation is the culmination of unchecked emotions that have gone unrestrained and taken over a person.

As an educator sharing some personal experiences from your youth and the accompanying emotions that you struggled with can be very instructive. Such transparency can gently impart truth through the backdoor without being preachy or pushy. Students love to hear of their teachers' childhood personal struggles. It makes them feel like their teacher is a real human being rather than a barking mean dog always bossing them around.

Conflict resolution techniques and approaches to resolve tension are innumerable. Share some of your personal experiences, open the classroom up for discussion, and teach your students some of your personal conflict resolution secrets.

Surely you have ways you deal with that relative you meet over the holidays once a year during family reunions. Maybe for you it is a coworker or a less than likeable neighbor. We all have somebody who rubs us the wrong way. Figuring out how to manage your emotions, guard your heart, and restrain your mouth around such people takes incredible discipline.

Please share how you do it, or at least provide us some entertainment by sharing your struggles and failures during your futile conflict resolution attempts. Both our successes and failures are equally instructive and enlightening for students.

Plus when you as a teacher open up as to your own personal failures, it makes students feel safe to do likewise and be transparent about their own struggles. This paves the way for true and heartfelt discussions on topics of interest for the entire class. Besides your classroom discussions could be the answer to a parent's prayers and transform a family.

Paul speaking to a lively crowd seated on the floor in India.

90. Teach Students Tolerance & Acceptance

Oprah recently did a show on children being "bullied to death" at school. Sadly two boys in middle school (both in different parts of the country) committed suicide after being continually harassed and called derogatory sexual names at school in front of their peers.

These boys being only eleven years old were of African American and Latino descent. The first played football and was a good student. The second enjoyed dancing and was a likeable boy. Yet in school a couple callous and cruel students thought it fun to participate in sexual slurs belittling them.

Although neither boy was gay, this is what a few cruel classmates were calling them. The Latino boy being from the Virgin Islands got made fun of and heard from his bully, "You're a virgin from the Virgin Islands."

What troubles me the most about these incidents is the tender and young age at which our children are now being forced by their peers to discover and defend their sexuality. I myself was a late bloomer and didn't hit puberty until I was about sixteen years old. Yet never did I get called a faggot or branded gay as a youth because I did not have a girlfriend. Honestly, I simply wanted to play baseball day and night. Girls weren't on my mind until about the eighth grade of middle school. Even then I was not pursuing girls. They were pursuing me.

Yet because of the lewd and aggressive sexuality splattered all over the media, children today are being confronted with adult issues before they reach the appropriate age to adequately understand and deal with them.

Such heinous in your face sexuality is mind boggling to tender hearted children who are disinterested in such things at their age. Understandably so and we as educators must protect them from sexual bullying and name calling, which often is far more hurtful than racial slurs.

As educators we must teach children about the importance of tolerance and unconditional acceptance. Diversity and difference should be celebrated. At the very least those who are not like us should be tolerated.

Every human being deserves a degree of common decency and personal privacy to live freely without hateful name-calling. Students however as we know can be cruel and hurtful to one another. Often it becomes so commonplace that educators can become immune to adolescent behavior.

Nevertheless there comes a place where the name-calling reaches a point of cruelty and is no longer fun. Playful joking can quickly get out of hand and become belligerent when it is intended to tear down another child. By no means should racial or sexual slurs be tolerated among your students.

The harmful psychological effects of such name-calling can be inwardly devastating for children and youth alike. We as educators must create a culture and atmosphere within our classrooms where tolerance is actively pursued and all people lovingly embraced.

Just because a student doesn't feel like he has anything in common with another classmate doesn't mean he has the right to belittle or degrade him. Mutual tolerance and acceptance must be taught and practiced in our classrooms. Moreover the self-esteem of each child must be built and cultivated so when such belittling remarks from peers come, children are secure in themselves and don't let such unkind words take root in them.

As for accepting each other, children must be taught they are free to disagree but should be encouraged in their disposition not to be ugly or disagreeable as a person.

91. Teach Responsibility & Respect of Parents

Too often the children and youth of this nation have been mesmerized by consumerism and comparison with the possession of their peers, by which they seek to manipulate and demean their parents when they don't get all of that which they want.

Yet we as educators must install within the youth of our country the importance of the greater values – love, honor, integrity, discipline, duty, truth, and respect. These must begin at home and be cultivated by their parents. We as educators in the classroom must reiterate and reinforce these values and uphold them above all things. Things in and of themselves cannot and should not be thought to add anything to our self worth. To lead children to believe things can enhance our identity is a gross deception and disservice.

It is the responsibility of teachers to cultivate self-respect among students and simultaneously encourage youth to respect their parents. The Bible itself says this is the first commandment with promise, stating that we are to honor our mother and father so that we can be given long life on earth and that it will go well for us.

Is it any wonder our nation has found itself in innumerable difficulties presently? The woes of our nation economically, environmentally, politically, and internationally (due to our past arrogance and alienation of the global community while we demonized and invaded other nations) has come back to haunt us. We are now dealing with blowback and the consequential repercussions of our past failures.

No Presidential administration is perfect, but without it being purposeful it is destined to fail. Sadly among all of our national and lofty initiatives, the simple foundational principle of honoring and respecting our parents has rarely been mentioned.

Beyond the debate for national health care coverage, few have dared to mention the importance of caring for our elderly within our own family. Asian and Latino families usually do so, but other ethnicities (particularly Caucasians) sometimes fail to see the value in our elderly.

This attitude explains why our nation has morally declined and violent crime is on the rise. With the departure of spirituality and the elderly, our moral compass and the values with which our national founding fathers birthed our great nation have also gone.

If we as educators fail to teach our students the importance of respecting their parents, those in authority, and the elderly: than we are opening the door for widespread rebellion and anarchy. If self is exalted and reigns supreme, human disregard will continue to escalate, and our cities will become overrun by crime.

By no means can a nation sustain itself without respectful law and order. Decency and basic human values therefore must again return to the classroom lest we as a nation collapse from within. More important than FCATs and standardized tests is teaching manners, decency, and respect. Because multinational companies will not hire educated idiots who lack social grace and manners.

I don't care how high a kid scores on his FCAT. If he doesn't have any manners or social grace, it is highly unlikely he will succeed in life. If schools only concentrate on grades and release reprobates into society, we have done our nation a great disservice.

I realize it isn't teachers' job to parent students. It is however educators job to teach students so they can succeed and survive in life beyond the classroom.

92. Teach Students About Health & Wellbeing.

One thing we must be alert and mindful of when teaching our students is the importance of proper hygiene and personal care. Upon beginning teaching, I noticed many of my students had heavy plague on their teeth. Being concerned and desirous of teaching them the importance of oral care, I mentioned the benefits of using dental floss.

Beyond brushing one's teeth, you'd be surprised at just how much plague dental floss can dislodge and remove from your teeth. Not only does brushing and flossing ensure oral hygiene, good breath, and a lovely smile; it also helps sustain your teeth for a lifetime. It is worth noting that without healthy gums, it is likely your teeth will decay faster and possibly begin to fall out.

Root canals can cost over $1,000 and can be very painful. I therefore would rather brush and floss regularly to save time, money, and prevent personal pain.

I also taught my students the importance of eating a sufficient amount of fiber daily by way of nuts, grains, fruits, and vegetables. I emphasized the importance of drinking enough water daily, without which their intestines could not be cleansed and their internal organs could not be sustained.

I asked my students, "What do you need to flush a toilet?" Some of my students looked puzzled (probably by the question as much as by the answer).

When I told them "water" the light bulb came on for many students. As water is to a toilet, so too is water to your body – needed to flush out toxins and waste. Otherwise we will eat more than we eliminate daily, which is one reason Americans keep getting bigger and increasingly obese.

I taught my students how long they could live without oxygen – 2 minutes. Therewith I encouraged them to protect their lungs and encouraged them not to smoke. Secondly, I asked my students how many days they could live without water – 40 days some estimate. Hence I emphasized the need of water, without which none of us can survive.

When some students remarked, "I don't drink water." I replied, "Yes you do. Whatever you drink has water in it as the main ingredient."

Such instructive and educational material will benefit students for a lifetime, while also blessing their families. Yet many of these simple truths and facts had never before been told to my students.

Our bodies should be our most cherished gift of all. Yet many of us neglect and abuse our bodies, never thinking of the repercussions and harmful side effects until we are ill and acutely suffering.

We would be far healthier if we would be proactive and cultivate healthy lifestyles rather than seek unnatural drugs and medicines to solve the damage done by years of bodily neglect.

As for the many learning disabilities doctors now medically diagnose children with and prescribe drugs for, most of them could be eliminated entirely if parents would feed their children living food without chemical additives that cause restlessness, brain fog, learning disorders, chemical imbalances and eventually cancerous tumors within the body.

Email me (info@PaulFDavis.com) for the one book and DVD I deeply feel educators and parents need to enlighten them on the dangers of food - "the new drug" – and how to safeguard their children from chemicals in foods that alter brain structures and hinder children's ability to learn.

93. Teach Sexual Sobriety & Abstinence

Alongside proper health, I often stressed the dangers of substance abuse to my students. I told stories of my mother, a cheerleader and honor graduate when she was in high school. She was popular and made homecoming court. Yet because of her lack of discipline, disrespect of her parents, and yielding to her foolish friends: my beloved mother at a young age began using drugs. Not long thereafter she became addicted to drug use and alcohol abuse.

Such stories ushered in a holy hush within my classrooms as my students intently listened to my own family's personal struggle with harmful substances. My transparency and willingness to be honest about these heavy topics opened up students to talk about their own struggles.

Some students began to mention and talk about drug dealers on campus, peer pressure, and situations they had dealt with within their own lives.

I am a big supporter of school uniforms. Removing the seductive tight and revealing clothing of our ladies on campus will greatly help keep hormones in check. As for guys, baggy and sagging pants (so low you can see a guy's underwear are unacceptable) are the rage among teenagers mesmerized by the hip-hop culture.

Some great places to get school uniforms and sports team apparel for your athletic department:
http://click.linksynergy.com/fs-bin/click?id=3RWH2TJD1YU&offerid=116553.10000207&type=4&subid=0

http://click.linksynergy.com/fs-bin/click?id=3RWH2TJD1YU&offerid=137999.10000028&type=4&subid=0

With all of the many sexual diseases being spread through intercourse among multiple sex partners, kids need to be forewarned and alert to the dangers of premarital sex.

During my first year teaching the swine flu epidemic swept through the world causing illness and death. New diseases such as these need to be understood so we can adequately prepare school staff to take every necessary precaution to prevent the spread of diseases.

Food born illnesses also are on the rise as are various viral infections caused by physical contact. Educators (like doctors and nurses in the medical industry) find it hard to avoid touching doors, classroom supplies, and other objects commonly used by students.

Kids coughing in your room and in close proximity to teachers makes it extremely difficult to avoid disease. Pharmaceuticals are very costly and not always covered by educators' insurance plans given by the school board.

Teachers therefore must understand medical ramifications and take every precaution within the classroom to minimize the spread of illness and disease.

For help along this regard, here is a very informative resource concerning medical conditions and illnesses to empower teachers and administrators to be on their guard against the spread of unwanted bacteria and infections in the classroom.

http://click.linksynergy.com/fs-bin/click?id=3RWH2TJD1YU&offerid=35400.10000022&type=4&subid=0

Below is a non-toxic, pesticide free head lice treatment for school kids that you can trust to detect, prevent & remove lice:

http://click.linksynergy.com/fs-bin/click?id=3RWH2TJD1YU&offerid=176018.10000010&type=3&subid=0

94. Teach Healthy Relationships & Boundaries

Youth can be a bit brutal and overly forthright when it comes to talking about the opposite sex. I was shocked the first time I substitute taught at a teenage mothers' school.

When one young lady asked what I typically do full-time when I'm not teaching, another female student shouted out, "He lays pipe."

This was my introduction into teaching high school within the state of Florida. Once I was teaching full-time at a Central Florida high school, I heard all kind of things I care not to repeat.

One young man overheard me speaking about what a fine job a female student did on her assignment. He shouted out, "Who is Rhonda? The girl with the big breasts?"

If you are teaching secondary education prepare yourself to hear these types of things from youth. The less outwardly you reveal your state of shock, the more quickly you can diffuse the tension and disarm hostility among students.

Nevertheless early on it is advisable to teach proper conduct, manners, and morality within the classroom. Let your students know from the get go what you expect of them and never accept anything less. Remember what you begin to tolerate will eventually tend to dominate among your students.

Therefore swiftly deal with inappropriate behavior and speech to nip it in the bud before it further blossoms and wildly spreads. The less often students see or hear inappropriate things the less likely they will be to entertain and participate in such crude behavior.

Strive to maintain your learning focus within an intellectually stimulating environment. As you interact respectfully and show your students by your own example how to address classroom visitors, school staff, and cafeteria workers: they in turn will learn by observing you.

Leading by example is most necessary for students who may have no example or guiding light at home. Given the rise of absentee parents, single parents, or parents working multiple jobs to sustain the family; we as educators must be willing to teach social grace and proper boundaries to keep our own sanity within the classroom. Otherwise there will be widespread pandemonium and unrest.

Boundaries are rarely taught in some cultures. Educators within the United States therefore must acquaint students to our societal norms, preferences, and nuances as a people.

Given that the United States consists of such a large landmass on which we its citizens dwell and live, it should be no surprise we get a little touchy when people invade our personal space. We as a people like our personal space and privacy.

Alternatively students from other countries are more accustomed to cramped quarters, sharing a room with a sibling, and showing patience to others waiting in line at the cafeteria. Certainly in this area Americans can learn from their friends overseas.

Perhaps a road trip in an RV motor home along with some outdoor camping would help us acclimate and warm up to being around people a bit more. This could work wonders for your disposition and bring your family closer together too!

http://click.linksynergy.com/fs-bin/click?id=3RWH2TJD1YU&offerid=170943.10000004&type=3&subid=0

95. Teach Successful Study Habits

When my father spanked me for bringing home a D on my progress report in 6th grade, he never sat down with me and explained how to study properly. I was disciplined and chastised for making bad grades, but never taught how to make good grades.

Too often parents and teachers tell kids what to do, but not how to do it. The best educators know how to not just lecture and preach sermons to their students about what to do, but take time to patiently instruct them HOW to do it.

If parents were challenged to teach their children how to do much of what they are yelling at them about, many parents would stop yelling and scolding their children. The reason being is few parents know how to get to their desirable objective. Few parents take the time away from their busy schedules, personal lives, and favorite TV programs to tell their children how to succeed academically.

Teachers therefore often have to pick up the slack. One algebra teacher with whom I worked told me stories of parents coming into his office screaming at him to teach their kids fractions. Yet his job description and assignment was to teach algebra.

Fractions are something students typically learn in elementary school. Parents therefore need to be proactive and ensure their children are learning the assigned material in school and not assume that just because they pass the grade, they are mastering the foundational educational material.

When parents make this deadly assumption and fail to work with their children academically, it catches up with their children eventually. Students cannot sleep and daydream in class for years and suddenly think when they get to high school they will be able to carry on in this manner and graduate.

All learning is layered, which means unless you lay a strong foundation upon which to build, you will eventually collapse from within academically. When a student fails to pay proper attention in class and merely considers the classroom a playroom to entertain himself and his friends, a rude awakening is soon to come when he has to repeat a grade and his peers pass on to the next level.

Parents who fail to plan for their children's education plan to fail. Children eventually pay a heavy price for their parents' neglect. It is far easier early on to become actively involved in a child's education, then to have to play catch up years later and reverse the curse of neglect.

Nevertheless with a spirit of faith and heartfelt patience educators and parents can together work miracles. Teachers however need to get parents in the game early on.

Teachers can do so by sending letters home with students to parents, phoning parents to let them know how their child is doing, and having teacher–parent conferences.

These things take time, but so does teaching fractions in a high school algebra class when a student is years behind. A few moments to write a letter, make a phone call, and meet with a parent will work wonders for your students.

When I had a student acting up in class and becoming a disciplinary problem, I phoned and spoke to his father. After having done so, the student's grades and conduct immediately improved. Thereafter I had no problems with the student.

That being said, ask yourself as an educator what takes longer: phoning and speaking to a child's parent for a few minutes, or taking a few minutes out of class every day to restrain an unruly child?

The latter is a far more painful and lengthy process. The most efficient use of your time as an educator is keeping parents informed and continually involved in their children's education.

Honor the child and praise them to their parents when they are doing well in your class. Begin on a positive note and acknowledge their strengths whenever you speak to their parents.

With my problematic youth mentioned above, I told the parent, "Frederick is a phenomenal young man and a joy to have in class. He has a lot of potential, but as of late he has been a bit distracted with his friends and is causing some problems in class. I would appreciate it if you could speak to him. I know he wants to do good for you and you want him to get a good education to ensure his future success in life."

What parent would resist or get angry about a request for help to ensure the well being of their child? Begin positively, acknowledging the child's potential, and ask for parental involvement.

This will make your life far easier as an educator, because discipline and punishment can only be measured out effectively at home by a child's parents. Inviting parents into the educational process is a win-win for everyone, cultivating mutual respect for all parties involved.

Paul & Karla with Paul's parents & maternal grandparents.

Paul with some boys outside of a school in Surabaya, Indonesia.

Indonesia is the world's largest archipelago with over 16,000 islands. The fourth most populated nation on earth and the world's largest Muslim populace, Indonesia is a wonderful place to visit on business or for a vacation.

Paul received open doors across many schools in the island of Java (Indonesia's most populated island), where he was invited to speak and inspire students and faculty alike.

Paul is a frequent guest speaker and often asked to provide faculty in-service training for educators.

To invite Paul to your city, school board, or campus write:

RevivingNations@yahoo.com

Within the subject of your email write: "Inviting Paul to Speak"

96. Teach Students Memorization Techniques

As a visual learner myself, I know the importance of comprehensible memorization techniques. Much of what is comprehensible within the chambers of a student's imagery is often not articulated verbally by educators during instruction.

Why is it when many of us spell words we look up? What is it we are looking for or at? Many learners have pictures in their mind they refer to when spelling words and recalling information.

Since much of middle and high school academics consists of memorization, why is it educators so rarely teach memorization techniques before requiring students to remember piles of information?

Undoubtedly this is one of the flaws of the educational process. Somewhere in the teaching process, educators must slow down long enough to teach students how to memorize and process the vast amount of information they are daily being given.

Otherwise students will experience information overload and eventually feel entirely overwhelmed. This is not our objective as educators. Therefore I suggest early on, if not on day one, that teachers take time to teach organizational skills and learning techniques.

By no means am I an expert on this, but I do at least recognize its importance. I feel it is our job as educators to do our best to instruct students in the secrets we used as students to quickly learn and process information.

Teach your students the test taking tips you applied during your education. Relate stories from your life. Be transparent and get into the minds of your students, asking them how they process and learn information.

When I received a D on my progress report in Science in 6th grade and got the beating of a lifetime from my dad, I quickly scrambled to learn as much as I possibly could in that Science class.

I had no idea how to tackle that body of knowledge, but I quickly learned. My next test was on the anatomy of the body, wherein I was required to identify and spell each bone of the body correctly.

I therefore locked my bedroom door, took the paper in hand I was to learn, and verbally repeated to myself over and over again the bones of the body, while looking at the diagram showing the location of each bone accordingly.

Instead of sitting at my desk, where I might have fallen asleep: I stood to my feet and walked back and forth in my room with paper in hand reciting the bones of the body. Verbally and visually (using two of my senses) I began to drive the data down into me, while reciting it repeatedly.

Then I began to put my hand over the name of each bone in the body to test my ability to remember the bone's name. After practicing this for several hours each day until I knew every bone in the body, I then began practicing how to spell each bone.

With a blank sheet of paper I wrote down every bone in the body. Without the help of the diagram given to me by my teacher, I would within my mind's eye visualize each bone and try to write it down (attempting to spell each bone correctly).

After going through this process repeatedly for hours and days, I eventually mastered the name, location, and spelling of each bone in the body.

When the day came to take my exam, I scored two 100s on each part of the anatomy test. That Science teacher awarded me the "most improved" student recognition at the end of the year. My dad's belt applied to the seat of higher learning worked wonders for my academic performance.

My improvement came as a result of studying, something I rarely did in 5th grade while in elementary school. Beyond my father's belt (his only contribution), I did everything else and somehow figured out how to study.

Other students are not so fortunate. Let us as educators therefore try to enter our students' world and understand how they best process information in preparation for a test.

It is worth noting, later in my life, I went on to work as a personal fitness trainer for some years. Therefore what I learned about anatomy and the bones of the body proved useful. I used the same learning and memorization technique when I had to memorize the muscles of the body prior to earning my fitness trainer certification.

If we as educators will take the time to teach our student acronyms, memorization techniques, and how to organize & process information: we will empower them for a lifetime of success academically and professionally.

Chinese students Paul taught English at Disney World over the summer with the Language Company in Orlando, Florida.

Friends Paul made in Burundi, Africa while speaking in a village within the war-torn nation. These handsome boys were very excited to see and welcome Paul to their village.

If you'd like to sponsor Paul to go to more remote villages throughout the world such as these, tax-exempt charitable donations are welcomed at paypal.com / RevivingNations@yahoo.com / or Dream-Maker Ministries, PO Box 684, Goldenrod, FL 32733

97. Know Student Learning Types & Tendencies.

As I mentioned before, I am a visual learner. Students differ in the ways they learn things.

President Abraham Lincoln read out loud so he could audibly absorb that which he was reading. By combining the visual stimuli of the words on a page with the audible pronunciation of those words, Lincoln actively engaged both senses to enliven his studies and educational absorption.

Other students are kinesthetic in that they need to touch and feel the subject matter. These students benefit from actually holding and feeling mathematical numbers. Calling kinesthetically inclined students to the board to work out their mathematical problems and write equations is also useful.

An interpersonal approach to learning could also implement a class role-play, where students go to the market to buy ingredients for a recipe they will later cook. Providing a limited budget with which to buy supplies can be a useful exercise to get students to awaken to the importance of mathematics and budgeting properly when allocating resources.

Through ongoing classroom interaction, teacher monitoring, and active observation educators can discover the learning types of their students. Thereafter teachers should model the lessons to actively engage each learning type throughout the instruction.

This will awaken each student and enliven classroom discussions ensuring a better learning focus. It is wonderful to suddenly see disengaged students come alive to the learning material and emotionally buy into the educational process.

Beyond seeing the value in the lesson being taught, students need to feel and connect with the method by which the subject material is being taught.

I know this can sound at times ridiculous and unnecessary for educators who immediately see the value in any lesson. For students however feeling and connecting with the material (along with the methodology with which it is taught) is inwardly important and allows for a greater level of emotional investment. All of these elements (tangible and intangible) increase both the stimulation and internal motivation of students.

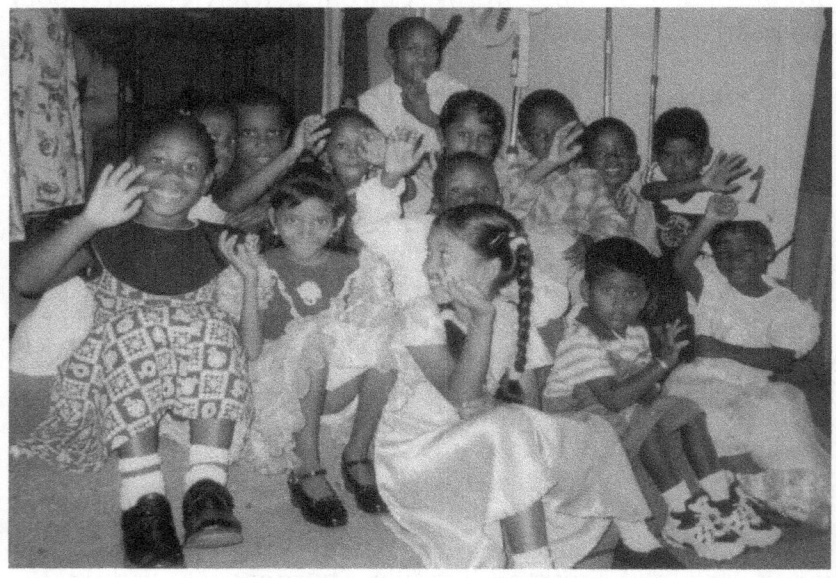

Beautiful children in Guyana where Paul spoke at a church in a very poor, remote area within the interior of the country.

It is said there is a high rate of AIDs and HIV within the nation of Guyana. Yet the people themselves are very lovely and kind.

Thankfully Paul's got durable luggage to endure all of the places he has been to during his travels. Get great luggage to meet your travel needs below at a very discounted rate.

http://click.linksynergy.com/fs-bin/click?id=3RWH2TJD1YU&offerid=81276.10000184&type=3&subid=0

98. Encourage Students to Travel

My world travels have provided me the greatest education of all. Seeing over 50 countries, more than 50 islands, and 6 continents has been the greatest educational experience I ever could have embarked upon.

Meeting new people, experiencing different cultures, learning about geography, eating various cuisines, learning unusual customs, and discovering unique faux pas have all been extremely enlightening.

No amount of books could ever have taught me these things – especially not me, I being a visual learner. Some things are more caught through interaction and observation rather than taught through books.

As an educator, one of the greatest things I have ever done is impart to my students the love of travel. As the world becomes increasingly interconnected and interdependent, global cooperation is no longer an option. It is a must and most necessary to the survival of us all.

No longer are we only in need of mutual cooperation diplomatically to sustain global peace. The environment and economy also require that we as nations work together.

My international students (who have come from afar to live in the United States, assimilate, and learn English) have been greatly encouraged by the fact I have traveled to their respective countries. Rare is it to find a teacher who has lived on foreign soil and traveled to all the corners of the globe.

This type of understanding learned from my world travels has enabled me to quickly connect through my own personal experiences and stories told in the classroom. Students love to hear a teacher tell of his or her experiences in their home country. It immediately removes walls and barriers to bring teachers and students closer.

Encourage your students to travel, learn another language, live abroad for the summer, and participate in an exchange program for a semester. These life experiences are invaluable and will be forever cherished by the brave students who dare to go abroad.

Students who have braved the seas and oceans that separate us to study abroad always return to their home countries greatly enriched and inwardly enlarged. Nothing cultivates manhood and womanhood within a student like living abroad apart from his or her family.

Once out of the comfort zone, we learn a lot about ourselves. Beyond the common and ordinary, we tend to discover new things about ourselves that shock and surprise us. We mature as we recognize areas in which we are weak and need to grow. As we arise to the challenge to overcome the circumstances in which we presently find ourselves, we can conquer all obstacles and come out from every situation stronger and wiser.

Traveling, studying, and living abroad will contribute to students' maturation; causing them to grow in strength and wisdom. Parents who are confident enough to entrust their children with such a life-changing opportunity and experience see boundless rewards.

Cultured and traveled children are more respectful of others and appreciative of what they have. Instead of being quick to compare themselves with others, they are more apt to humbly embrace everyone and develop meaningful relationships from the inside out.

Materialistic youth who merely live in America and take their parents for granted would greatly benefit from a cross-cultural experience in which they lived in a poor country for a while. Then they could awaken to their arrogance and callousness of heart by which they alienate people.

Lectures and instruction alone (whether by parents or teachers) will never prove sufficient to bring youth to the realization of that which they foolishly take for granted everyday.

Global travel has a silent way of teaching youth some of life's most important values without you ever having to open your mouth. If you truly want your students to mature into respectful adults and global citizens, encourage them to travel internationally and experience our world.

The smallest plane Paul has ever flown in thus far, an eight-seat Peruvian plane. See the cockpit and the pilots flying up ahead. The pilots passed back the boxed breakfasts upon take off.

For 24-hour turnaround time on getting a passport try:
http://click.linksynergy.com/fs-bin/click?id=3RWH2TJD1YU&offerid=140795.10000018&type=3&subid=0

Compare hotels and save:
http://click.linksynergy.com/fs-bin/click?id=3RWH2TJD1YU&offerid=163355.10000029&type=3&subid=0

99. Encourage Students to Do Internships

As my high school students got closer to graduation I encouraged them to apply for prestigious jobs and internships.

WhiteHouse.gov

CIA.gov

FBI.gov

UN.org

NSA.gov

Microsoft.com/college/ip_overview.mspx

Disney.go.com/DisneyCareers/wdwcareers/hourly/index.html

NBCunicareers.com

If you don't take chances, you won't make advances. I therefore always encourage my students to take risks, try new things, and be adventurous when it comes to pursuing their dream job.

Following your heart when it comes to your career can be life changing and transformative. Amazingly, many people have never been brave and bold enough to go after what they want in life. Therefore they get out of bed every morning to do jobs they dislike. Miserable, they make everyone around them miserable.

I encourage my students to follow their bliss and throw caution to the wind. This I have done in my own life, which has always proven to be the path of least resistance and produced the greatest successes for me.

To not follow my passion and dreams would be to violate myself. I therefore always purposefully move forward to whatever is burning inside of me. Even if I only manage to attend to my dreams an hour or two a day (because of having to temporarily work a job to pay the bills), I nevertheless pursue my dreams diligently. I will lose sleep before I let my dreams fall by the waist side and die. For me to live abundantly, I must follow my passion inwardly.

Sadly many do otherwise and live with regrets all of the days of their lives. I don't want this for my students. I therefore always endeavor to breathe life into their dreams. I encourage you to do likewise.

There are enough negative people and dream killers in the world. The least thing students' need is a teacher who doesn't believe in them. If necessary walk by faith, not by sight, as you assess a student's potential. After all, when you believe in a student you give him reason to believe in himself.

Paul with youth from church he lovingly led for three years.

Great travel rates to help you spend less and travel more below:

http://click.linksynergy.com/fs-bin/click?id=3RWH2TJD1YU&offerid=128469.10000022&type=4&subid=0

100. Encourage Community Service to Give Back

Encourage your students to in some way give back every year. Perhaps you might want to suggest they befriend a new student who just moved to town or transferred to school from another neighboring school.

Visiting the elderly in nursing homes, comforting the sick in hospitals, feeding the hungry, clothing the poor (with the excess clothes in the closet they never wear anyway), and befriending orphans are all excellent ways to give back.

Victims of local or national tragedies also need our support. Supporting a local charity can be a great way to start. Showing love to those most in need around about you in your immediate neighborhood also can make a world of difference for somebody.

By teaching students their duty to give back, it causes them to be more thankful for that which they've got and embrace their responsibility as a citizen in their community and nation.

When students become proactive and use their talents to serve others, this makes the world a better place for us all. By teaching students to think beyond themselves, you open their minds to a whole world of possibilities.

Awaken leadership within your students and cultivate creativity wherewith they can contemplate ways to make a difference in the school and community.

Students where I taught recycled to help the environment and raised money for a variety of charities throughout the year. It was inspiring to see students doing good and making a difference.

Student led food drives, fundraising, volunteer work, and activism always results in leadership development and enhancing youth's problem solving skills.

When we give we always live. It is somewhat supernatural how when we give, our hearts within truly feel alive and abundantly live. I suppose when we are being a blessing it reminds us how blessed we truly are.

Oprah and *People magazine* recently collaborated on a show honoring hometown heroes making a difference in hard times. One man started a *Good News Garage* to help single mothers without transportation get cars to be able to get to work. With the generous donations of people in town who gave their used cars to the garage, he was able to fix them up and gift them to the mothers in need.

A medical doctor in Eureka Springs, Arkansas with the help of his church provides free healthcare to the poor who are in need of medical attention.

A couple in South Dakota that own a small hotel took the initiative to begin housing poor homeless families who were freezing in the cold and without shelter.

Two small girls with big hearts began giving socks to keep the homeless folks' feet warm during winter and donated toys to kids who had lost their homes in sudden fires.

Such random acts of kindness and human generosity should move and inspire us all to do something no matter how small. Begin where you are and make a difference everyday in somebody's life.

Educators may not have a lot of money, but they can give of their heart and time to neglected children. The many coaches who teach sports to students are worthy of great honor and recognition for the many sacrifices they make to nurture maturing youth on the ball field.

Listen to your heart and follow your inner inspiration. As you do, you will be greatly blessed while being a blessing to someone else.

Paul with his buddy Bill on a mission of love in Jamaica where they led a group of young adults to give back to those in need. The two guys took a moment to temporarily kidnap the donkey at the compound where they were staying, which they put in the bedroom of the girls to give them a good scare.

The greatest scare however came when a girl named Michelle (who usually spent an hour getting her makeup on every morning) got in bed and upon crawling beneath the sheets found a huge bullfrog Jamaic-ing her scream real loud!

Paul always likes to have fun while he gets any job done!

101. Value Youth & Future Leaders Over Money

When you feel discouraged, used, and abused before you quit consider the impact you are having on the youth. Remember our nation's future (and the future of the world) is found in our youth.

Although administration and your fellow teachers may not celebrate you, if the kids do, then rejoice! Your students as an educator are your world. Forget and don't pay attention to noisy negatives from elsewhere.

More valuable than money are the precious souls you are teaching and empowering for the future. Never underestimate the power of your influence to mold and shape the precious minds of your students.

Know assuredly in the heart of God and your students you are somebody. Don't allow financial dictates and fears to constrain your gift as an educator, which is flourishing and nourishing the students sitting at your feet daily to be taught.

Uphold and honor yourself even when nobody else does. Often teaching is seemingly a thankless job. Yet you are as a modern day missionary, a Mother Theresa, pioneering a path of hope in a dark and disillusioned world mesmerized and disoriented by the demands of the day.

Let your light shine therefore ever so bright knowing that you may be the only source of illumination in your school today. We all have bad days, but thank God for somebody who breaks forth into joy nevertheless and chooses to reverse the curse with thanksgiving and rejoicing.

Be that shining light today that others draw near to for inward illumination, inspiration, and hope. Set off a chain reaction of thanksgiving and appreciation.

Turn all darkness into light and overcome evil with good. This is why your heart has drawn you to be an educator.

Although it at times seems overwhelming and too much to ask of one person, as you pray for resurrection power and walk forward with childlike faith, you shall continue to rise above your difficulties and magnificently become great.

Your greatness is already within. Just cultivate it daily and let it manifest for all to see.

Take a checkup from the neck up! Renew your mind and pull up that spirit inside. Be a resourceful and powerful educator that can overcome any conflict and setback.

Pioneer a path of success for your students and fellow educators to follow behind. Be a servant leader that always loves and lifts those around you. Quell all gossip by refocusing and showing them a better way!

Be better than that and overcome every setback with a faith filled smile!

Fast forward a bit in your mind to the future and see grateful students sending your Thanksgiving cards telling you what an impact you made upon their life. Imagine what it will feel like when you receive an invitation to many of your students' high school and college graduation ceremonies.

See them running up to you with tears in their eyes and giving you a great big hug, thanking you for believing in them when nobody else did. Hear them now saying, "Thanks for believing in me, when I didn't even believe in myself. You truly made a magnificent difference in my life. Today I owe much of what I am to you!"

102. Enjoy Your Holidays & Summer.

As I approach the end of my first year teaching at the writing of this book, let me tell you I am excited about my summer. Having free time to enjoy during holidays and the summer is one of the best things about being an educator.

When those weekends, holidays, and the summer rolls around, don't you get entangled with extra duties. Take time for yourself and live your life abundantly.

You can always get more money, but you can't get more time. Your life consists of time. Therefore use it wisely. There is no better or wiser use of time than enjoying your life fully.

Sadly many people work like a beast of burden and never take time to enjoy their lives. Not me! I'm going to work hard and play hard!

As an educator we know you work hard. Now for goodness sake, you give yourself some time to recreate, take a break, and play for a while. Rest, recuperate, revitalize, and renew yourself however you please. But take time to enjoy the wonderful pleasures of life.

If you've never been on a cruise before, consider accompanying me on a fabulous cruise. Bring your friends for additional fun or if you fancy to go alone to relax happily do so.

If interested write me at RevivingNations@yahoo.com providing the following information:

1. Available dates for travel

2. Budget

3. What you want to see & experience most in your life.

4. Smoker or Nonsmoker

5. Health - poor, average, good, excellent

6. Number of people traveling with you.

7. Destinations you are most interested in seeing.

I'd love to hear from you! World travel is my personal passion. Inspiring people to live their dreams is my joy. Therefore I'm often speaking on cruise ships to empower people just like you to be their best.

What more could a person ask for? Inspiring people an hour or two a day and seeing the most beautiful sights on earth is a dream come true for me!

I can't get enough of it! I know you'd enjoy it yourself and we'd have a blast.

Depending on your budget and desires, I can try to design something especially for you. If you are flexible and adventurous, there is a strong likelihood I can exceed your expectations and surprise you!

Paul in Germany on the 3rd floor with the kids
in a stunning home near the border of France.

103. Master Emotions & Outward Reactions

En route to mastering your emotions and outward reactions as an educator, learning how to establish rapport is a vital skill that will eliminate much tension in the workplace and within the classroom.

Knowing how to establish rapport, win friends, influence people, and get what you want in life is surprisingly something rarely taught throughout all levels of education.

Rapport can be established several ways:

1. A warm smile feels good both for the giver and receiver.

A smile is the least expensive thing you can give, which imparts the valuable and priceless feeling of loving acceptance.

A smile costs nothing, creates much, and enriches those who receive it without impoverishing those who give it.

2. Take a genuine interest in others.

"I" is the most common word used in the English language. Never forget to give place to the almighty "I" when interacting with others. Listening to others is loving.

3. Ask questions about others.

Questions open people up to talk about themselves, which we all love to do.

4. Help and serve others in what they're doing.

Educators are usually extremely busy people. Everybody could use a helping hand once in a while. A sure way to make friends and influence people is to serve them in whatever they're currently doing.

5. Put sunshine on your face and soul into every handshake.

Beyond a welcoming smile, give a hearty handshake or affirming pat on the back when appropriate. Within the southern states here in the USA, men don't typically shake the hands of women (which many educators are).

Given the possibility of sexual harrassment charges and making someone feel uncomfortable, a smile might be the best approach when dealing with ladies (until they extend a hand). For men however a hearty handshake, brotherly knuckles, a high five, or pat on the back can be a form of encouragement.

Be aware of the nonverbal body language coming from a person, particularly their facial expressions. Some of your fellow educators are not bright eyed and bushy tailed in the morning. Give them some space and don't be overly verbose too early in the morning (until they get their coffee). Others just like personal space and quiet all day long. If so, endeavor to give them what they want without intrusion.

Adapt your approach according to the person, be it a coworker or student, you are interacting with. Students too require some personal space and respect, without which they may become inwardly rebellious and uncooperative.

So use some finesse and tact to skillfully woo students to participate in class and complete assignments. Sometimes you have to appeal to their ego and interests, making them feel like they are in control and at liberty to decide what they want to do. Ultimately they are. However upon going home, many youth quickly learn the board of education applied to the seat of higher learning works wonderfully to produce a cooperative and attentive student within the classroom.

Therefore do not hesitate to phone the parents of your troublemakers in the classroom and ask them to get involved in the disciplining of their child. You will be glad you made the phone call and usually see a remarkable difference in the child thereafter.

6. When you meet somebody do so enthusiastically with animation.

Whatever you do or say, do so wholeheartedly. Don't just go through the motions. Be animated and exhuberant in your affirmation, praise, and performance. As you do, your passion will grip the hearts of those around you and win their affection. As you remain consistently positive, those who question your sincerity over time will realize you're genuine.

7. Don't prematurely judge and try to size up people. Believe the best about everyone.

Beware of hastily assuming you know all there is to know about a child. Usually a child's home life and family surroundings have shaped them to be a certain way. Reconditioning and mentally repositioning them will take time. Therefore be patient and gentle as you await the internal adjustment.

8. Never put your map on people.

As hard and challenging as it may be, allow others to be without you putting your map upon them. Life is meant to be an exciting journey, discovery, and adventure.

Don't kill the adventure and joy of the journey by revealing your insights about a student or coworker prematurely. If they are not intuitive enough to ask or inquire for your insight, what you know and tell will not likely be well received.

As the Chinese proverb goes, when the student is ready, the teacher appears.

Therefore show restraint and hold back deeper revelations about a person and their pursuits until they invite you to speak into their life. This will prepare the way for you to speak to a tender heart after circumstances and life's experiences prepare the soil of their heart to receive the seedlings of truth you deposit.

Remember it takes time for a farmer to cultivate soil, as circumstances beyond our control are often at play. Trust the workings of life to have their way in people's hearts and reveal the special secrets to be discovered by them over time.

Enjoy the journey of life and avoid the temptation to be overly anxious. Irrational exuberance can lead to many painful consequences. Therefore take a deep breath and let life move at its own speed.

Sometimes the wisest thing you as an educator can do is exercise patience, wherewith you slow down to the speed of life. Like the river that flows on its own accord, some things do not require you to push to make them work.

Just simply do you part daily and trust the process to gradually work its wonders within your students. One day you will wake up and show up in the classroom, where you will see a sudden transformation in a student. Over time each student (according to his or her own timetable) will experience a similar metamorphosis as you continue to nourish academic growth among all of your students.

It will be like the farmer who scatters seed in the field, after which he happily sees a mighty harvest spring up before his eyes. Therefore when it comes to small beginnings with your students, such incremental and progressive steps never despise.

As you remain consistent to fulfill your role as an educator and trust the process, weekly learning gains and progress will occur in your students causing your heartfelt dreams as a teacher to be gloriously realized.

Therefore continue to believe even when you see no outward evidence, because inwardly within the hearts and minds of your students you are working miracles daily.

104. Promote Word Power & Creative Expression

When I assigned my 11th and 12th grade students the task of writing their own individual resumes, I was surprised to see how little vocabulary was used to describe themselves in this personalized exercise.

After a few days of further coaching and instruction, eventually the students felt free enough to use their creativity to express and adequately describe themselves to a future employer.

Unfortunately years of conditioning by the American educational system tends to constrain young minds more than free them. As an educator, you therefore need to teach creative thinking and problem solving. Unless our nation's youth learn how to express themselves verbally and in writing, it will be extremely difficult for them to excel and succeed in life after graduation.

To simply give multiple-choice (also known as multiple guess) tests, educators are doing their students a gross disservice. Although such tests may be faster and easier to grade, they also derail students from thinking the answers through and answering to the full extent of their ability.

Open-ended questions therefore are necessary and ideal to facilitate meaningful learning. Meaningful classroom discussions, thorough examination, in depth reasoning, thoughtful dialogue, and coherent written expression all need to be facilitated and encouraged.

Outside of the four walls of our schools, life is not going to be a multiple-choice test. On the contrary, real life demands heartfelt thought and decisive action. Otherwise we shall spiral in circles without any personal progress.

105. Understand & Empower Gender Awareness

Beyond racial, ethnic, and religious discrimination: we must remember gender discrimination is still alive in America. Women still earn less financial compensation than men in many occupations, although they do the same job. This professional inequality in the workplace is disturbing and needs to be further addressed.

A national conversation and reformative legislation must go forth to change the way women are valued in society. Inequality economically is equivalent to institutionalized racism, which hinders and removes financial opportunities from capable people. Such must be confronted and corrected.

106. Know How & Where to Ask for Help.

Be careful who you ask for help as a teacher. Some people obviously won't want to be bothered and will simply complain about you to others when you make a request.

Get your bearings and get to know people with whom you work. This will take a while in the beginning. Yet once you know who is willing to help you and who is not, do your best to seek out help from those who genuinely are willing to answer a question or provide a few minutes of their time to assist you.

Grumpy people on staff tend to demonize others and make small requests into something much larger than it really is. Therefore avoid such people and save yourself much hardship along the way.

Everybody has a specific assignment and you never know the extent of somebody else's workload. Therefore always be respectful and don't overstep your boundaries.

Whenever you manage to get someone gracious enough to help you, be sure to thank her for helping you. Thereafter reciprocate whenever you can when you are asked for help.

107. Keep it Simple for Substitutes

The truth is most substitutes are not looking to make a career out of teaching (some are retired). Many just want to fill in the gaps for teachers, give the kids an assignment, and relax.

Don't expect substitutes to explain every nuance about the subject material to your students in your absence. Keep it simple for your substitutes. Most importantly, be sure to give them enough work to keep your students busy (even the advanced kids who get their work done in a flash).

Don't draw out a lengthy and complicated lesson plan for them. Make it easy to understand and follow. If you have any special instructions or forewarnings to give the substitute that will also help.

Perhaps you will want to alert the substitute to a particular student who has been disruptive and a disciplinarian problem. If so, have the substitute notify you of any difficult students that cause trouble in your absence.

Have the substitute communicate to students your expectations and how you intend to deal with any arising problems in your absence once you return.

This will keep the kids alert and remind them that you will soon return.

Be sure to thank your substitutes for filling in for you. Otherwise they may think you are a bit rude and insensitive. Do your best to appreciate your substitute teachers, making them feel welcome whenever they are serving at your school.

Before you go away (or if you know you are sick and will be absent) clean and tidy up your room for your substitute. Nobody likes working in a messy and filthy workspace. Get yourself and your room together before bringing guests or substitutes in. That being said, tell your students the usual class rules also apply for substitutes teaching in your absence.

108. Recruit Student Leaders in Each Class

Each of your classes will have more progressive and dynamic students that shine. Providing these students are likeable and well mannered, you might cultivate them to be your assistants in some respect in class.

Assuming they don't mind working with you or perhaps being labeled a "teacher's pet" for doing so; you might request a couple advanced students to help the others in their assignments (designating what students they are to help or work with) in return for extra credit.

Other students may not excel academically, but perhaps may be well behaved. Some among this group may want to help be your eyes and ears concerning disciplinary matters related to proper behavior in the classroom.

Each class has its own feel and mannerisms. Therefore be attune to what is going on around you and upon developing a trust and affinity for certain students, you might entrust them with some small responsibilities to help improve academic performance and behavior in the classroom.

Paul with the youth group he led in Oviedo, FL.

109. Classroom Management with Wisdom

Managing and controlling a classroom full of wild young students is no easy task. Harnessing them the minute they walk through the door is vital to your success when it comes to classroom management.

I immediately endeavor to get all students to be seated and focus on the task at hand for the short time we have together during class (50 minutes for the six classes I had each day, along with a 50 minute planning period).

What makes classroom management difficult is when students lie to you and betray your trust. I can immediately cite three instances where students looked me right in the eye and lied to my face.

One student neglected to write their name on their assignment, which they had done a pretty good job on and completed in a timely fashion. When I taped the completed no-name assignment to my white board, one young man not long thereafter claimed it was his.

I later realized he lied to me. The completed assignment was not done by him and therefore did not belong to him. Upon asking the assistant principal how to handle the situation, I was advised to give the lying and cheating student a zero for that particular assignment.

I did so. Incidentally, that student never blatantly stole anybody else's work again. Neither did they lie to me thereafter (to my knowledge).

Another student lied to me in class saying, "Mr. Davis, I need to eat. I'm hungry. My doctor says I need to eat."

When I replied, "You are welcome to eat in 50 minutes when the bell rings and we all go to lunch."

The student replied, "My doctor says I need to eat. It's important that I eat."

I then responded, "If you can provide me a letter from your doctor saying you need permission to eat in class, I will allow you to do so. Otherwise if you cannot provide a letter from your doctor or guidance counselor permitting you to eat, then you like all of the other students cannot eat in my class."

The student then replied, "My doctor died. I can't get a letter."

Another student of the same nationality as the two mentioned above (I wont disclose the national origin lest I be accused of being racist, which is impossible since I've traveled to this particular country and have some wonderful students among this ethnicity.) came to me at the end of lunch when she saw me with a milk carton in my hand.

"Mr. Davis," she said, "can I have your milk? I did not eat lunch."

I replied, "You didn't eat lunch?" I was nearly ready to give my milk to her when I noticed the expression on her best friend's face. I then asked her best friend, "Did she eat lunch?"

The best friend revealed she did eat lunch and in fact was lying. Upon catching the student in a bold face lie, I remarked, "So you're lying?"

Unfortunately too often this is how students play their teachers to see how far they can get with them and to what extent they can get stuff from them. Therefore be discerning. Ask a lot of questions. Move slowly. Think things through thoroughly.

Embrace fair measures and standards of equality. Be on your guard for emotional manipulation tactics, which when you yield shall quickly be followed by other students' complaints of unfair treatment and inequality.

110. Tell and Show Students You Love Them.

I met a young man in Singapore who expressed to me that his father had never before told him that he loves him. Although the young man knew by his father's actions that his daddy loved him, something inside of the young man longed and yearned to hear it verbally.

Because of the multiplicity of our senses, we all long for love to be communicated on many levels. The more levels we can show and express our love for someone, the deeper and greater the emotional connection.

To withhold love from a child (even unknowingly) can cause children to feel a bit empty emotionally and drive them to do unseemly things to fulfill their need for love. Unbeknownst to some parents, even teenagers want to hear that they are loved.

Although teenagers pass through the season of seeking to establish their identity (however fragile it may be) and gain the respect of their peers, true stability emotionally is cultivated and found within the family structure. Parental affirmation and approval more than anything else emotionally stabilizes a child.

Despite children's efforts to be cool and liked by their peers, a parent's approval comforts and assures a child more than anything else. This is why the parental relationship is so vital to ensure academic success. Because if a child is not emotionally secure, the inner restlessness and yearning for affirmation will drive him or her to misbehave in class to get peer approval (if not at the very least attention – no matter how futile it may be).

By communicating your love for your students as a class periodically and frequently, you can endear them to you as their teacher. Let's face it, not every teacher communicates their love for their students. Some see teaching as just a job and a way to pay the bills. Others teach because they have no other professional skills or experience.

When you as a teacher break the mold and show some emotion, it will open up your students to you. When a student feels loved, respected, and appreciated he or she will seek to please you.

Students enjoy interacting with teachers who genuinely care about them and have their best interest at heart. Participating in classroom activities with teachers who care is fun and emotionally enriching for students.

Teachers who love their students frequently communicate such by praising them during classroom discussions, questions and answers, and throughout every piece of the required assignments. The result is students respond wholeheartedly and actively become engaged. Teachers who pull students by their heartstrings always outperform teachers who bully and push students to comply with rules and procedures.

Living and leading from the heart both feels better and produces far more than being a dogmatic disciplinarian. Kids want to feel your heart and sense you sincerely care for them. When they do, there is nothing for you they will not do.

Love, honor, respect, and cultivate your students' potential. You are a winner and a vital component to your students' lifelong success. As you go from surviving to thriving as a teacher, your level of joy will increase and your students learning will as well.

Your best days and most blessed days are ahead of you! Thank you for reading this book and investing in yourself as an educator. The word is a better place because of you!

If this book has helped you, I'd love to hear from you. You comments and suggestions are always welcome.

Your friend for success,

Paul F. Davis

The last day for me as a teacher, before leaving the school I served, I wrote a letter to the staff saying thank you. That letter is here below.

Good morning administrators and teachers,

Just a brief word of thanks for all you've done this academic year noticed and unnoticed.

As a first year teacher within a public school, I had no clue what I was getting myself into. I thank [Principal's Name] for not telling me when she hired me. That being said I thank [Teacher Mentor] for enduring me through the transition process.

Whenever I felt like quitting, all of the teachers' ongoing dedication was a great source of motivation. Those who offered a friendly smile along the way are most appreciated.

Thanks to [ESOL Department Chair Teacher] for mentoring me and teaching me how to use the computer operating system and all the many websites (twice …as once the tech guy took my computer during the virus scare I was a bit clueless the second go around).

Thanks to [Assistant Principal's Name] for providing clear and concise instructions verbally and in writing (Oh yeah, and a million thanks for sacrificing your weekends to slave away at all of those football games to make money for the school. Sorry I couldn't make it as I was fighting my insurance company and using rental cars for 4 months after a drunk driver totaled my car.).

Thanks to [Dean in charge of substitute teachers] for covering for me when I was sick. Thanks to [lunch attendant] at lunch for always smiling and [lunch director] and the culinary staff for serving us meals daily.

Thanks to [Librarian] for being a source of stability in the media center and allowing me to use his printer nearly all year long, as mine was out of business until nearly the end of May.

Thanks to [Librarian Assistant] who sings like an angel and her son [Name] who always met me every morning with a smile and something funny to say to make me laugh, along with some brotherly knuckles and chuckles.

Thanks to all my friends whom I lunched with in the cafeteria.

Thanks to [School Nurse] for taking care of my eye when I brilliantly banged it against my out-of-order printer atop my bookshelf and had to go to the ER. Thanks to [Principal's Secretary] for patiently enduring me when I got perturbed at the insurance company who wanted me to drive over an hour away, while injured and bleeding when there was an ER within 10 minutes. She magnificently sweet-talked the insurer to allow me to go to the nearby ER.

Thanks to all of the deans who kindly came to my class to remove disruptive troublemakers hindering us from staying on task academically. Thanks to all the wonderful guidance counselors who masterfully deal with our students many emotions, while silencing their own when they feel overworked and overwhelmed.

Thanks to the "glory girls" at the front office, the gatekeepers if you will (You know who are you are!).

Thanks to [Soccer Coach's] coaching and leadership for speaking into the lives of the young men on his team. I enjoyed teaching many of them English and witnessing their character being daily constructed and strengthened.

Thanks to [2nd Assistant Principal] for being a gentle and unassuming man who provides a phenomenal example of leadership daily.

Thanks to [Veteran Teacher Next Door] for caring, inquiring, and providing a sympathetic ear.

Teaching at [School Name] has been an amazing and life-changing experience.

Although I shall not be returning next year to be a teacher, I will happily carry on in the spirit of service as a speaker & minister.

Wishing you and your families all of the blessings of heaven and earth!   ….and a fabulous summer! Now get out there and enjoy it!

Paul :o)

Ps. Please stop calling me Mr. Davis.

Pss. Please don't reply to me here [school email] because it has been said "he doesn't check emails." LOL

Try: RevivingNations@yahoo.com

www.PaulFDavis.com

www.DreamMakerMinistries.com

www.itietheknot.com

www.new-teacher-success.com (check back in August)

Paul in Ft. Lauderdale trying to avoid getting a big head.

The following below is a heartfelt (and rather long) letter written to the Florida Commissioner of Education by Paul.

June 2009

Dr. Eric J. Smith, Commissioner of Education
Turlington Building, Suite 1514
325 West Gaines Street
Tallahassee, Florida 32399

Dear Commissioner of Education, Dr. Eric Smith,

I am writing to present to you some concerns related to compliance with *"Equal Access to Appropriate Instruction for English Language Learners"* as required by Florida law's administrative code 6A-6.0904.

As a native born Floridian, I can honestly say (as you well know) the demographics of our State are truly changing. I recently heard on the radio that here in Orlando where I live, Caucasians now account for about 49% of the local populace (no longer being the majority). That being said, as we happily embrace diversity, educators too must change with the times if we are to be relevant and remain effective.

As a first year teacher of English Language Learners (ELLs) in the State of Florida, I served [Name] County's [Name] School during the 2008-2009 academic year. I was entrusted with the care and education primarily of 11th and 12th grade ELLs (along with a few other 10th grade ELLs).

As a worldwide speaker I traveled to over 50 countries and taught international students English for nearly three years before beginning to teach in the State of Florida as a substitute teacher in Orange County. Upon applying for the English Students of Other Languages (ESOL) teacher position at

[Name] School, I was hired by Principal [Name]. Having never worked in the public school system, I had no idea the extent of the paperwork and administrative duties that juxtapose with teaching.

Shortly after being hired to teach, I was hit by a drunk driver on a Tuesday afternoon in Volusia County on July 8, 2008 and my car was totalled. As for me, I also sustained bodily injuries which I am to this day struggling with. Following this accident that demolished the one car I and my wife drove, being without little money, we were forced to drive a rental car until November 23, 2008, when we finally secured financing to buy a 2006 Hyundai Sonata. Incidentally, exchanging rental cars every week or so was extremely challenging emotionally and logistically on my marriage – not to mention financially. Meanwhile I continued to visit doctors and battle my insurance company to recuperate money to buy a replacement vehicle.

Little did I know how under prepared and over my head I would be upon taking this teaching position. I had no idea how much administrative work was involved beyond my daily teaching duties. Furthermore I was a bit behind upon beginning, because after being hired [Name] County School Board's personnel investigator was concerned I might be a sex offender (given that two other men bearing my name in Illinois and Nevada were on the sex offender registry) and required me to stay off the school premises until I had been cleared to begin my employment. Nevertheless after establishing my good name and confirming my innocence during the investigation, [Name] County School Board and Principal [Name] graciously gave me the opportunity to serve at the school under her care as an ESOL teacher.

Given my many personal struggles, which came upon me unexpectedly as mentioned above, I was unable to serve in a volunteer capacity at athletic events and school fundraisers. Nevertheless I was never forced by my principal or any administrative staff or fellow teachers to participate. Yet in a staff meeting my principal did mention this is something she gives strong consideration to when renewing annual contracts. Irregardless, this is not why I am writing.

In regard to the laws, policies, and practices of being an educator within the State of Florida I am undoubtedly a novice. That being said, I do not know all of the ins and outs of educational legislation, initiatives, and mandates. Instinctively however I felt a few things might not have been right as to the way I was trained (or not adequately trained) as a first year new teacher serving ELLs. That being said, I probably failed to take the initiative at times to pursue such training early on, due to being already sufficiently overwhelmed with teaching itself, learning the new computer operational system necessary to fulfill my role as a teacher, and endeavoring to complete required professional education (all while battling my insurer and attending to my physical condition as mentioned above).

Since the Florida Department of State: Florida Administrative Code amended and passed 6A-6.0904 in May 2009 concerning *"Equal Access to Appropriate Instruction for English Language Learners"* (Rulemaking Authority 1001.02, 1003.56 FS. Law Implemented 1003.56 FS. History–New 10-30-90, Amended 5-7-09*)*, school districts, principals, and teachers might need to be made more aware of what is required of them in regard to ELLs.

On that note, the Florida Department of Education might also benefit from being alerted to possible violations of *"Equal Access"* to ELLs. Perhaps by establishing lines of open communication concerning the implementation and enforcement of the new rule, school districts, principals, and teachers can be fully made aware and thereby be more apt to comply.

By no means am I trying to cause trouble for my school district, former principal, or fellow teachers at my school. I deeply admire, love, like, respect, honor, and appreciate them all for their contribution as educators preparing our next generation of leaders.

Yet I share a similar love and respect for the ELLs whom I teach and know are immigrating to live and be educated here in the great State of Florida. Among my concerns pertaining to *Equal Access to Appropriate Instruction for English Language Learners*, I would like to bring to your attention the following:

1.   To the best of my recollection, a written ELL Plan was never given to me by the school district or school where I taught, upon beginning work as an ESL teacher. Although as an ESL teacher I was "appropriately qualified" and experienced in keeping with section 6(b), item 2 of the code; I cannot honestly say I was properly trained by the school district or school for the position before commencing teaching in the public school system.

My teacher mentor is a very kind, humble, and knowledgeable lady, who was helpful answering most of my questions. Yet being a new teacher I was not always knowledgeable as to what questions to ask to enhance my teaching and classroom instruction. My principal reviewed my lesson plans once early in the year and made some helpful comments. My teacher mentor's comments however proved to be the most helpful, as she encouraged me when summarizing my lesson plans to not ask "what" questions, but rather "how" and "why" allowing for more thought and feedback from students. The only disheartening thing about this wonderful advice is I did not receive it from my teacher mentor until May 1st, 2009. Although my teacher mentor made herself available to help throughout the year, sometimes a new teacher may not realize he or she is off track. Such instances requires a teaching mentor to be a bit more proactive.

Nevertheless a new teacher can only bear so much early on and perhaps my mentor in her wisdom gave me some space lest I feel overwhelmed during the initial demands of getting adjusted as an educator. I therefore choose to believe she took the right course of action in my regards. However for other new incoming teachers, such might not always be ideal.

2. The area of most concern for me is section 6(b), item 4 pertaining to "utilization of native language materials" which I later learned from my ELLs near the end of the academic year that they were being deprived of. Specifically, the bilingual dictionaries were unavailable in many of the ELLs classes and the bilingual dictionaries provided had a limited amount of vocabulary.

For example, a student by the name of _____ from Cuba informed me that he was struggling with the vocabulary in his health class. Upon evaluating the vocabulary _____ was being tested on, most of the words were not in the Spanish-English bilingual dictionaries used at our school. I informed _____'s health teacher that he would need a medical bilingual dictionary to be adequately equipped for her test as the school provided bilingual dictionary was greatly lacking in vocabulary. To my knowledge no other bilingual dictionary was provided.

The Haitian paraeducator at our school who assisted me with the ELLs immediately noted upon arriving that the Creole-English dictionaries given to the Haitian students were greatly lacking and significantly smaller than the Spanish-English dictionaries. He suggested the Haitian students be given French-English dictionaries, which also were unavailable.

When I mentioned to Mrs. _____ (the head of the English department) and Mrs. _____ (the head of the ESOL department) that the concise Haitian-Creole dictionaries are substantially smaller than the Spanish-English dictionaries (both coming from the same publisher), both agreed but mentioned the purchasing of dictionaries is something that occurs at the district level.

For a clear visual of the dictionaries in comparison see:
http://www.youtube.com/watch?v=1KgrHP9ivtc
http://www.youtube.com/watch?v=7qgVM1rvL3E

Among the students' written complaints I received and hereafter provide (as stated in their own words and sometimes a bit grammatically flawed) are:

> "I didn't pass four classes because there was no bilingual dictionary. The teachers don't provide with solid information for the Spanish speakers. The teachers that don't have dictionary are Mr. _____, Mr. _____, Mrs. _____, and Mr. _____." -- Puerto Rican student

> "I want to let you know that in my Reading Class, there are no Spanish-English dictionary. I find this really unfair. Please do something about this situation."
> -- Puerto Rican student

> "I don't like haitian dictionary because I cannot find all words I need and I don't understand the word the writing in creole that why I don't pass my reading fcat. The fcat word not even in the dictionary. How going to pass the fcat if I don't understand what the word say."
> -- Haitian student

> "The things I hate about the Haitian Creoel-English Dictionary is that the words are not correct and some of the words I look for are not in there. For example "Discrimination" that word is not in the Haitian-English Dictionary. All I want is a Better dictionary and more words in the Dictionary. In this Dictionary some of the creoel words are wrong and I need for them to be better.

The word rude – in creoel the dictionary put grosye and salute – they put salye." -- Haitian student

"I have a big problem with Intensive Reading class because I don't have a Spanish dictionary and I don't speak English very well. So I need help sometimes, but I never find it. This is the only class that I am failing and I don't know why. I just want that somebody help me to pass this class because I have a good record and I don't want to bring my grades down for one class. Also I have some articles in the class that are too hard for me. For example, 'fertilization in-vitro' are words I don't have a way to translate. I hope that somebody will help me to pass that class which is so painful for me. I have"
-- Cuban student

3. Another concern in the ESL program is when hiring native speaking aides, we must remember many of these aides still have accents from their native tongue. While the native speaking aides are a great help to ELLs, their accents can sometimes be a hindrance to ELLs of other ethnicities.

For example, a bright Chinese exchange student was tested by a Hispanic native speaking aide (a paraeducator serving the ESL department) upon arriving to our school from China. The student told me during the verbal test, the native speaking aide pronounced "three" as "tree" (among other words) further complicating the difficulty of the test and hindering his level of performance on the exam.

4. Instructions for administering FCAT testing and empowering ESL teachers to proctor the FCAT also could be improved.

The day before giving the FCAT to ELL students, I had some brief questions I sought to get clarified by my principal following some emails I had received and read from her. My principal however firmly told me to read the email I had been sent (which I already had), she being confident it would answer all of my questions. Upon asking my teacher mentor, she assured me not to worry by informing me the instruction and guidelines to follow would be given to me the day of the FCAT, a script of sorts, which I could follow when giving the exam. I have attached that script for review.

On March 10, 2009, the first day I ever gave the FCAT to students, when following the script verbatim, I stopped as indicated at 11:20am waiting for the verbal directive from my administrator over the intercom. The verbal directive never came and an hour later when my principal showed up in the room to which I had been assigned and saw my students not testing, she began to rebuke and chastise me. Another discipline session occurred after dismissal of students in my principal's office at the end of the day, wherein several deans were sat behind and around me in intimidating fashion (one of whom later resigned for being relationally involved with a student). I was never asked to speak and share my perspective concerning the incident, just sign a document after listening to my principal's characterization of the events. I therefore feel my voice should be heard.

Although the ELL students were to be taking an untimed test and should not have been stopped, I was strictly told to follow the script. While I admit to my error in stopping my ELLs during the FCAT, the contributory negligence and impatience of my principal by which she refused to answer my questions the day before further complicated the matter, which could have been answered and clarified rather quickly had she taken a few moments to do so. Thus, I the ESL teacher proctoring the exam and my ELL students were put at a great disadvantage during the FCAT test taking process.

5.   Some ELLs are disciplined and sent to "choice" (being made to leave their class) for speaking in their native tongue. English speaking students who speak socially during class are not punished in a similar fashion.

An intelligent female Mexican student informed me that Mrs. _____ sent her to "choice" (discipline room outside of class run by the academic deans) for quietly speaking in Spanish to a nearby friend after she finished her work. The student told me that other English-speaking students, nearby who had also finished their work, were permitted to speak quietly to each other in English. When however the Mexican student conversed in Spanish with her friends, she says she was disciplined and sent to "choice" for alleged bad behavior.

6. Equal access as communicated in section 1(a) and 1(b) I feel was denied my 11th and 12th grade ELLs (and the few 10th grade ELLs I also taught), specifically "equal and comparable in quality to that provided to English proficient students". Section 1(b) mentions "equal and comparable services to those provided to English proficient students on a timely basis", which I feel the below mentioned scenario falls short of.

My principal remarked on my teacher evaluation at [Name] School in May of 2009 that I do "not read emails in a timely manner or follow instructions given in written form". Yet my principal herself, my teaching mentor, and the technology director all received emails from me during the first week I began teaching in September, 2008 (and thereafter) requesting assistance to make the smart board in my classroom available for use. I even used a subject in my email to get everyone's attention saying, "Smart board, dumb teacher." I wrote the email on September 15, 2008, which I have attached for review.

I however was told the smart board technology and components to make it work were unavailable and would later be provided. Unlike other English teachers without ELLs, I taught the entire academic year with a smart board in my room that I was never able to use. The smart board's accompanying components to make it work were never provided.

In regard to the allegations of "not reading emails in a timely manner" and not following written instructions in written form, I have provided two examples of poorly written instructions by administration and a third example documenting administration's neglect of an email request for direction in regard to dealing with sexual bullying on campus.

1. The March 10th, 2009 FCAT event procedures stated at 11:20am: "Session 2 should be finished" and "all test books and answer books are to be put in the envelope". The 11:30-12:10 instruction stated: "Students in Building 3 with extended/untimed tests and who have not finished testing will be relocated to the Media Center during this time."

   Although I followed the instruction to "finish" testing at 11:20am as told to do within the script, no administrator came to relocate the students during the 11:30-12:10 time frame. Upon arriving well after 12:10 the principal endeavored to correct the administrative error (after causing more delays by freaking out and refusing to listen to me concerning where unfinished students' envelopes were located, within which were their tests) and relocate the students to the media center to complete their tests, the majority of whom went without lunch to complete their exams. On that note my teaching mentor, the career counselor, and dean over substitutes did a phenomenal job working through the situation and assisting the students complete their FCATs.

   The assistant principal also did a great job of remaining calm while bouncing me around like a tennis ball from building to building in submission to my frantic principal giving commands. Eventually my principal calmed down long enough to let me tell the assistant principal where the unfinished students' envelopes (within which were their FCAT tests) were located.

Thankfully administration corrected the FCAT test taking scripts for the following days, which clarified the instructions for the 11:20 time frame specifically stating ELLs were to continue without stopping (with the exception of permitted bathroom and lunch breaks) until they completed their tests.

2. On Friday May 29, 2009 I received an email from our school's director of guidance (sent at 2:40pm on May 28th after teachers' 2:30pm contract time is over and many have left for the day), requesting that all student elective request forms be alphabetized and returned to her upon completion. However on the morning of May 29th over the intercom, the principal instructed for the elective forms to be given to the office receptionist. This is just another example of administrative miscommunication, internal incongruence, and poorly written instructions.

3. When I wrote our school's director of guidance on May 8th, 2009 an important inquiry concerning sexual slurs and bullying occurring on campus (which Oprah had ironically just did a show on which led to two children committing suicide), I never received a reply until June 4th, 2009 (nearly a month later as evident in the attachment for review). Moreover my question was never specifically answered and the school's bullying procedures never provided for direction.

Therefore it seems only fair administration should itself read and respond to emails in a timely fashion and reevaluate its own internal incongruence and problematic written instructions before chastising teachers for noncompliance. Nevertheless over time I began to sense my principal's strong leadership and approach to discipline of students was becoming a bit bordering bullying toward her teachers on staff.

For example, early in the year the track coach confided in me during lunch one day saying our principal had referred to some aspect of his teaching as "queer", which bothered him. I actually stuck up for my principal at the time and spoke highly of her, hoping to persuade him from leaving and seeking a teaching position elsewhere (which he had mentioned).

Another instance occurred in a teachers' meeting during which our principal somewhat braggingly made mention of the frightened reaction of a particular teacher who's classroom she had visited during evaluations early in the year. Yet instead of assuming my principal took some perverse pleasure in intimidating her teachers, again I tried to give her the benefit of the doubt thinking that she might have brought it up for a laugh in humorous fashion or to relieve the tension of teachers. However later in the academic year when I heard from the track coach that he had been hospitalized for stress related migraines (something my teaching mentor also mentioned suffering from), I began to think maybe my principal's leadership style was such that it was driven and motivated by fear causing a multiplying effect resulting in some staff being a nervous wreck.

I empathize with my principal because while completing a form one Monday morning in her secretary's office, I overheard my principal tell her secretary that she actually got some sleep that weekend (something she said she often had trouble doing because she was usually such a "basketcase").

I cannot fathom the endless and many demands placed upon a principal, which heavily burden one's soul and leave little time for one to rest away from work. Such a troublesome load on one's soul leads to misery and endless suffering emotionally for us all. Because when one of us suffers, we all suffer.

My one year teaching taught me to honor and esteem principals to the same degree as pastors and law enforcement who direct and protect us. Besides working for my principal sometimes felt like I was in the military. Her job certainly looked very stressful from the outside looking in. Therefore by no means am I trying to belittle, demean my principal, or roll her under the bus so to say, but rather plead for somebody to help her better manage her emotions for her own personal well being and those who serve under her leadership. I would hate to see her have a heart attack (or give somebody else one) and die prematurely from all of the stress she is under.

To regain focus on the matter of "equal access" I'd like to mention something that occurred in my classroom one morning, when I had some unexpected visitors arrive in the middle of my class. When a distinguished lady with a doctorate visited my class early in the academic year alongside my teaching mentor asking me if there was any way in which she could help, I simply said: "Yes, you can ask the powers that be to give me the technology so this smart board works."

My teacher mentor apparently did not like it that I said this and replied: "I guess you've dropped the gauntlet."

Yet in no way was I endeavoring to be combative. I simply was crying out for help to whomever would listen. Sadly, nobody listened. When the Teacher Resource Specialist from [Name] County School Board came to visit me in my classroom in the Spring of 2009, asking me how I was doing and if I needed anything, I said with watery eyes: "The only thing I ever requested, which still has not been done, is to fix the smart board in my room so my students and I can use it."

Mr. _____, probably the most genuine and heartfelt person I encountered during my time working for the [Name] County School Board, said he would talk to our school's assistant principal. The assistant principal visited my classroom shortly thereafter and was evaluating the ceiling, most likely assessing the structural layout in order to install the necessary technology. Incidentally, I really like our assistant principal and the deans who serve at _____ School. Nevertheless I completed the teaching year without use of the smart board in my classroom.

Certainly as the school year progressed, the national economy further declined, and the educational cutbacks deepened; I thought perhaps the smart board technology was not being provided due to financial constraints. I therefore rarely said anything about it thereafter unless asked by others how they could help me. I didn't want to be a burden or cause any more hardship.

I sent several emails about the printer that didn't work in my classroom to our school's tech guy throughout the year, who was always cordial and did visit my classroom a couple of times, but never succeeded in repairing my printer until around May 22, 2009. Therefore I was without a smart board and a printer most of the academic year.

The media center director kindly allowed me to use his printer the entire year until my printer was provided. Thankfully I did have one white board along the side wall, which after repositioning all of my desks and chairs we were able to use. However had we been provided full use of both boards within the room as repeatedly requested (and many other English teachers had), ELLs learning opportunities could have been greatly enhanced and improved.

As a visual learner myself, I greatly benefit from visuals and overheads and know this to be true for my ELL students endeavoring to learn a new language. During our annual research project, one of my students from the Dominican Republic asked me if she could do a power point presentation and put it up on the overhead as in another teacher's class.

Unfortunately, I had to deny the request because we did not have the technology, neither the screen to visually show a presentation of this sort. Hence technology to integrate into the academic focus and learning was denied me the ESL teacher within my classroom.

The Canadian Education Association states in their book *"Teacher Working Conditions That Matter"* published in 2007 and available at the Education Resources Information Center website:

> To advance understanding of the issues concerning teachers' working conditions, the Elementary Teachers' Federation of Ontario commissioned one of the authors to do an analytical review of literature on teachers' working conditions. This resulted in the publication, *"Teacher Working Conditions That Matter: Evidence for Change."* The framework for this report is based on the premises that teachers' feelings and knowledge are the immediate "causes" of what teachers do and that many of these internal states are significantly influenced by the circumstances in which they work. Evidence points to the influence on teachers' work, and in some cases, also on student learning, of eight specific internal states: (1) Individual sense of professional efficacy; (2) Collective sense of professional efficacy; (3) Organization commitment; (4) Job satisfaction; (5) Stress and burnout; (6) Morale; (7) Engagement or disengagement (from the school and/or profession); and (8) Pedagogical content knowledge. The analysis identifies the working conditions which evidence suggests have a significant influence on each of these internal states.

By no means do I want to harm or jeopardize the jobs of the fine administrative staff mentioned above. In fact I believe the demographics of our D grade School requires a leader with the temperament of our able principal. Certainly she has done a fantastic job with discipline and governing the student body so as to ensure an ongoing rigorous academic focus. Moreover our principal has done an outstanding job with the athletics and innumerable extracurricular aspects wherein the students at the school now excel.

Know therefore my intent in submitting this letter is not to undermine or harm in any way the wonderful and goodhearted people serving among the fine administrative staff at _____ School, but to simply be heard (something my principal's personality type, a bit domineering and intimidating, did not afford me as an educator on staff).

Often we see things not as they are, but as we are. This is my concern for our principal. Sometimes children demonize their parents; students their teachers; and teachers the principals they work for. Yet this is not my heart and intention. I have malice toward none and charity for all. My hope and prayer is that the Department of Education and the county school districts can implement ways and means by which hard working and proven principals like _____, new incoming teachers, and ELL educators can all receive the support they need to succeed.

To further elaborate on the personality of my Principal (she who threatened to call police to arrest graduating seniors if they wore sunglasses when receiving their diploma), her final evaluation of me as a teacher made mention that sometimes I am "too strong" when dealing with matters out of my control. Of that I agree as it pertained to insurance monies being withheld without my authorization from my first paycheck (when my family was suffering the most financially following a car accident) and months later when I sustained a job related personal injury at school in February 2009, for which I was initially told by the school board's insurer to drive to a hospital over an hour away (with a bleeding laceration above my right eye) when there was a nearby hospital within 10 minutes of the school where I taught.

I exercised the same level of strength and resistance, when I arrived home the afternoon after completing work following being injured on the job and received a phone call from the county school board's insurer aggressively telling me that I must drive to _____ County from Orlando (where I live) to take a drug test the same day or I would not have a job. Thankfully in this matter I prevailed and was able to persuade the insurer to find a medical provider within 15 minutes of my home to take the drug test, which I did the same night.

Therefore only in matters of extreme personal importance was I "strong" and understandably so. As for my classroom demeanor as an educator I was deemed "satisfactory" in all parts of my evaluation as a teacher on my principal's final performance evaluation. If you would be so kind to inform me how to go about adding these comments to my principal's evaluation for the record, I would like to do so.

For the sake of ESL teachers and ELLs across the great State of Florida (and my predecessor at _____ School), I feel I owe it to all international students learning English in America and their families to write this letter. It seems only fair and right that all academic administrators and county school boards should provide international students (ELLs) the same educational opportunities, technology, and structurally equipped learning environments as English proficient students receive without prejudice.

I therefore with a clean conscience, seeking no personal aggrandizement, or vengeance humbly submit this letter to document my experience during my year of service as an ESOL teacher at _____ School. If I am inaccurate, incorrect, or ill informed concerning the above; I will happily embrace a rebuke and your correction. If however I am justified and accurate in the insights provided here above, I wholeheartedly entreat and urge the Florida of Department of Education to take every precaution to ensure the international students (ELLs) attending our State schools are provided equal access as required by law.

I deeply hope the day will come in America, where all English language learners (ELLs) who have come from beyond our borders, will happily and willingly stand to say the pledge of allegiance before school knowing that truly equality, liberty, and justice is for all.

In keeping with section 2(f) "the Commissioner of Education shall develop and implement standards and criteria for evaluating the appropriateness of basic ESOL instruction in each district."

I pray you may have God's wisdom from above to rightfully discern the details of said standards and criteria for equality of instruction, the implementation of which shall greatly affect ELLs throughout our State schools.

In conclusion I entrust this matter to you with heartfelt gratitude and appreciation for your service to the State of Florida, our schools, and students' education.

Respectfully yours for the furtherance of Florida and all learners.

Paul F. Davis

PO Box 684

Goldenrod, 32733

RevivingNations@yahoo.com

www.PaulFDavis.com

Although that letter was lengthy, I think it is useful to get an inside look at what principals, administrators, teachers, and students are saying. All points and perceptions are valid. We therefore want to examine each angle and aspect of education so as to better understand one another, be aware of our mutual objectives, and cooperatively work together to achieve success.

Invite Paul to speak in your city to inspire, motivate, encourage, comfort, and strengthen your teachers.

Support the professional development of teachers so they cannot just survive, but wholeheartedly succeed. Encourage aspiring teachers entering the educational profession so they can be equipped and empowered to flourish as educators.

Paul can also do book signings, breakout sessions, workshops, consultations with school boards, school leadership, and inspire staff to cooperatively work together with enthusiasm.

Enhance your educators' performance and productivity by investing in their emotional wellbeing and professional development. Transcend conflict at the workplace. Achieve internal congruence and interpersonal relational synergy among educational leaders. Clarify your purpose, articulate the vision, and build a team of educators desirous of experience dream fulfillment.

RevivingNations@yahoo.com

407-967-7553

PaulFDavis.com

Paul signing books for eager youth in Indonesia.

Paul's other Books and often requested speaking topics:
- Overcoming Adversity
- Breakthrough Leadership
- Diversity, Multiculturalism & Global Cooperation
- Academic Success for Better Grades
- Think About It
- Substance Abuse Prevention & Drunk Driving Detour
- Sexual Assault & Date Rape Prevention
- Healthy Relationships
- Breakthrough For A Broken Heart
- Empowering & Liberating Women
- Conflict Resolution
- Life Balance
- Reflection, Peace & Patience
- The Beauty of Life

…and many more!

www.PaulFDavis.com

www.ingramcontent.com/pod-product-compliance
Lightning Source LLC
Chambersburg PA
CBHW032036150426
43194CB00006B/305